TRILOGY

COINS & COFFINS

DISCREPANCIES AND APPARITIONS

THE GEORGE WASHINGTON POEMS

by Diane Wakoski

COINS & COFFINS

DISCREPANCIES AND APPARITIONS

THE GEORGE WASHINGTON POEMS

GREED: PARTS 1 & 2

INSIDE THE BLOOD FACTORY

GREED: PARTS 3 & 4

THE MAGELLANIC CLOUDS

GREED: PARTS 5–7

THE MOTORCYCLE BETRAYAL POEMS

SMUDGING

GREED: PARTS 8, 9, & 11

DANCING ON THE GRAVE OF A SON OF A BITCH

DIANE WAKOSKI
TRILOGY

COINS & COFFINS

DISCREPANCIES AND APPARITIONS

THE GEORGE WASHINGTON POEMS

1974

Doubleday & Company, Inc.

Garden City, New York

3/1974
am. Lit

COINS & COFFINS

CONTENTS

DISCREPANCIES AND APPARITIONS

CONTENTS

THE GEORGE WASHINGTON POEMS

CONTENTS

INTRODUCTION

This book represents the first three published collections of my work, *Coins & Coffins; Discrepancies and Apparitions; The George Washington Poems.* For the past several years they have been available only on the rare book market, and while I appreciate a reader who will pay from fifteen to fifty dollars for a book of my poems, I do not think anyone should have to in order to read them. Therefore, I am grateful to Doubleday & Company and to my editor there, Sally Arteseros, for making this edition possible.

I put collections of poems together as if the collection itself were a long poem. It is always a challenge to find a new structure, a new possibility of combinations. When I first started thinking of a book of poems in 1960, I had been writing for six or seven years and had been publishing my poems in magazines for about two years. I wanted to put together a book of poems constructed from dream images and brilliant and beautiful visions of the painful real world. Even though I also wrote discursive prosy metaphysical poems, and short fragmentary word-image poems, the poems I cared most about and felt most in touch with then were the poems which used one dominating image for their structure, which depended on a personal narrative describing a bizarre and terrifying world. The persons in the poem were always dramatic, as David in "Justice Is Reason Enough," or exaggerations of real people, as Elizabeth in "Elizabeth and the Golden Oranges." There was a sense that in our imaginations we are dramatic and spectacular people, and the poem was there to yield the imaginary life to the reader; at best to contrast or blend it with the mundaneness of reality.

I see myself as writing several different kinds of poems. I do not see my collections of poetry as "progressing" to different modes of writing, but each book as developing one facet of the kind of poetry I write. I have always been concerned with the metaphysical presentation of the real world, of the use of image as narrative and structure, of poems as dramatic speech, with poetry as the creation of a personal mythology, and the use of beautiful lyrical language for its own sake. I would like it if the reader could see in each book a predominance of the use of one technique or kind of structure for the poems. In *Coins & Coffins*, the poems could often be called surrealist in style, though their purposes are very different from a Surrealist Manifesto concern for poetry—the random use of image which leads each reader to his own separate interpretation of cognitive meaning for the poem. My poems are always selective, and I the poet am always busy trying to tell you what I think and feel about the world. In *Coins & Coffins* much of the world vision is structured around dream image or the associative process. But a goal I think you can find in all my poems, in all the collections, is to plead with the world, with the reader, with the person the poem is addressed to, to be kinder, more compassionate, more understanding, more intelligent. My poems are often about the pain I feel and they are a plea to the world to relieve it.

The George Washington Poems are all poems in which I address some man in my life as well as his alter ego, George Washington, a mysterious mythical figure, both representing the world I live in, "the man's world," with its militaristic origins and the glorification of fact over feeling. Many of the poems in this collection are comic and intend to present a vision of reality as absurd and foolish, often taking the dignity out of history in order to rewrite it. I think "George Washington: the Whole Man" is a kind of summary poem presenting both my own love and admiration for George and the men he reminds me of as well as my feelings that somehow we have all been swamped by history and bamboozled a bit; that its elegance is also an absurdity. That our feelings which we honor, simply because we have them, are also mundane and foolish.

Creating the self (and its attendant world) as mythology, allows us to laugh at ourselves, to satirize our own world and to see how passionately we can be devoted to its silliness.

Discrepancies and Apparitions is a collection made up of three smaller manuscripts originally. There are poems in it, like "Apparitions Are Not Singular Occurrences," which build around a dreamlike image in order to present a painful reality that, if described in everyday terms, would seem mundane and unworthy. It has always been a premise of mine in writing poetry that the poet has the same experiences everybody else does, but his technical challenge is to invent some imaginative way of talking about these problems, these realities so that they can be taken seriously. It does not really seem like a big deal to anyone else when you say a man or woman you loved betrayed you. So what? Everyone sometimes feels betrayed. However, that's precisely why it is so important for the poet to find a way to say it. I believe in the use of extravagant surrealist imagery, like the girl riding naked on a zebra wearing only diamonds, as a way of making the reader accept the specialness of the feelings of the speaker in the poem.

There are also poems in *Discrepancies and Apparitions* which use repetitive narrative to change words around until they present a construct of ideas. A poem like "Incident of Cherries and Peaches" poses a language problem like the difference between Alice in Wonderland's "I say what I mean" and "I mean what I say." I call these my metaphysical poems and they use as a structure the presentation of some real-life real-world observation and try to turn it into a statement *about* life as well as a statement *of* life. In all of my collections I have presented some poems which contain characters from my personal mythology—George Washington, Beethoven, the motorcycle betrayer, Daniel, David, Jennifer Snow, the King of Spain, etc. I write in the first person because I have always wanted to make my life more interesting than it was. So I created a Diane whose real experiences were dramatized and exaggerated, were presented as surrealist experiences or metaphysical ones, who involved herself with imaginary people who often had the characteristics of real people but were more interesting and mysterious. Perhaps I have always been the isolated lonely person living around dull or sad people, and the poems were a way of inventing myself into a new life. I do feel a strange connection with the worlds I have created and the people in them, though I do not really feel they are me or my world. It has been my obsession to try to see and understand the world truly. But that means seeing it over and over again, with all its changes, its attendant contradictions. I am never satisfied with anything I see but must keep inventing and reinventing ways to understand it.

Diane Wakoski

COINS & COFFINS

This Book Is Dedicated to La Monte

TOUR

Enter this room, if you will,
but silently.
It will seem empty,
but a white fox
and a black fox
are mating
on the crimson rug.
A number of gold appointments are featured
in this room
which you must not touch,
and the furniture is too valuable
to sit on.
However,
we do understand your wish
to see this place,
to breathe the incense,
and to appreciate its tradition.
If you are interested in the black fox
or the white fox
you may inspect them closely
and ask me any questions
you may have.
Notice the vividness of this place
and the faces that watch you
from the corridor lamps.
It is my pleasure that you are taking this tour.
I will be happy to tell you
whatever I know.
I hope you will not be alarmed to learn
that you may not leave this place again;
because you have seen the black fox
mate the white,

6

and to satisfy your curiosity
let me say,
both animals are now
dead.

DARK WINDOWS

The windows of my house are dark,
for a hawk has spread his wings over them.
I am frightened of the dark
and step out the door.
On to my gloved arm, I lift the hawk,
gently folding his outspread wings,
touching his feathers, soft as wind.
His body, feather-packed and tense with hooded fright,
makes only minute connection with my own—
his talons as separate metal hooks touching
what they must to hold, but yielding nothing
of the rust-feathered body.
I unveil the bird,
though the windows of my house are still dark.
He sits in tense immobility
and then
as sudden as a gust of wind,
he pecks out my eyes like two cherries.
I am blind,
the windows of my house forever dark. My arm
does not flinch from the rigid bird
gripping its leather branch
and again,
again,
he furiously darts at me, taking pieces of flesh,
stinging chunks in his scissored beak
from my face,
my neck,
my uncovered white arm. Then, his fury spent,
and the smell of warm blood soothing his microscopic strained
        nerves,
I feel the weight of soft feathers released against
my covered arm
and nestle against my bleeding face.

8

Quiet is the wind.
The windows of my house
may be always dark,
but inside there is light enough for any man
to meet his own
needs.

DIALOGUE

If you function nearly as well as my stuffed animal,
please tell me. I have often felt you inferior.
              The watchbird is watching you.
The next time it snows, please tell me.
              The watchbird will be watching.
And when a blue tiger stalks the forest,
he will have a marigold in his mouth.
              The watchbird will be watching.
Great god, who is this watchbird?
              He is a blue tiger.
With a marigold in his mouth?
              Yes.
              There is snow on the ground.
But why are we watched?
              Because of the circumstances.
              A blue tiger with a marigold
              in his mouth, walking softly
              on the snow; it is suspicious.
Can it be real?
              Of course not. There is snow.
Snow is real.
              Not in a jungle.
And the marigold?
              Exactly. Can you tell why it ought to exist?
I can't say why a blue tiger should,
or why there is snow,
and a marigold is even more confusing.
              Perhaps we need a girl.
Why?
              If there were a girl, she could be leading
              the blue tiger, carrying the marigold
              in her hand and walking barefoot in the snow.

But why is this more meaningful?
        Love, of course.
        Girls lead their fancy
        that flowers in the absence of life.
And this is more meaningful?
        Certainly.
        When did a blue tiger ever walk
        through the snow with a marigold
        alone?

JUSTICE IS REASON ENOUGH

He, who once was my brother, is dead by his own hand.
Even now, years later, I see his thin form lying on the sand

where the sheltered sea washes against those cliffs
he chose to die from. Mother took me back there every day for
over a year and asked me, in her whining way, why it had to
        happen

over and over again—until I wanted
never to hear of David any more. How
could I tell her of his dream about the gull beating its wings
effortlessly together until they drew blood?

Would it explain anything, and how can I tell
anyone here about the great form and its beating wings. How it
swoops down and covers me, and the dark tension leaves

me with blood on my mouth and thighs. But it was that dream,
you must know, that brought my tight, sullen little

brother to my room that night and pushed his whole taut body
right over mine until I yielded, and together we yielded to the
        dark tension.
Over a thousand passing years, I will never forget
him, who was my brother, who is dead. Mother asked me why
every day for a year; and I told her justice. Justice is
reason enough for anything ugly. It balances the beauty in the
        world.

ELIZABETH AND THE GOLDEN ORANGES

I

In packing boxes of spiders and amber,
under old letters, the stiff smell of folded satin
greets me tonight, in these quiet rooms:
a house dead, one that has never had life.
How proud my parents were of the wedding
pictures, their daughter in straight folds of silk—
if not beautiful, straight and clean: and the groom,
a man, that if they did not like, they had
to admire. How far all that is away.
The ink has turned brown; why do I open
these tall crates? So much unfulfilled time
has elapsed. My own hands are spiders
touching the satin, making webs from the box.

II

Zeno, with his arrows, saying they always
occupied a finite amount of space and proving
their static condition, disallowed progress
or change. He did not believe it. He saw
men live and die, not dying the same size
or in the same condition—baby-fine hair
turned to coarse hanks, milk coming from a cow's eating grass.
      He could not
believe, but wanted to know; arrows do not always reach
their targets. That is all I know. Not why
or how they get from one place to another.
The stiff smell of old satin greets me tonight.

III

Once married. Throw away twisted gold rings.
Cast them to the wind. Let spiders weave webs
about them, to glitter in the sun. Even a good
man would rather have a beautiful woman
than one who is not. She can stare in the mirror—

first lilies of the valley and April snow—
all day long and never turn a hand because
men love women who are beautiful, the bird
that flies out of an orange when you open
it. Who is the bird flying out of the orange
when you open it? There are so many birds.
The arrow does not progress, Zeno says;
but he sees the change in a man's hair.

IV
In packing boxes of spiders and amber,
you will never uncover the bone; the satin
is not stiff with blood but age. The arrow fell short.
There is bitterness in having only one chance
at your mark. Better to have never shot
at all. How often does a spider weave
a web? There is only one bird in every
orange. Leave gold rings at the circus.
Do not uncover the things you regret. My own
hands are spiders, crawling over this satin
handling letters that crackle like bones,
thinking of oranges from Spain
whose flesh is more fragrant than mine ever was.

AFTER LOOKING AT A PAINTING OF THE CRUCIFIXION BY AN UNKNOWN MASTER OF THE 14TH CENTURY

It is not so much
that he was a good man,
betrayed by his friends,
or killed by the stupidity of his time.
Hanging by his side are two other men
equally betrayed—
how else were thieves caught without fingerprints,
lie detectors,
or the FBI?—
equally brutalized,
equally suffering;
but the incredible and stiff soreness his arms must have felt,
the pain from bending backward at the elbow,
at being skewered with crude metal,
the feet crossed and plunged together with a nail.
The pain he felt
could not have had much to do with right and wrong.
The pain could not have been greater for him
than for those other two,
the thieves also hanging
by their own flesh,
gradually being ripped open
by the gravity that inevitably
pulls down.

Your painting makes me furious—
describing spiritual pain,
when the man was being literally torn open
without anaesthesia.
If he felt joy in that,
his mind was perverted:
are you describing joy as the perversion of pain?

Gold
is embossed on his robes:
honor.
Thirteen-hundred years late.
I rebel if you are telling me that
after the fact
there is nothing but honor.
Now,
seven-hundred years later,
I ask you something more,
being young,
but still remembering those yellow stars that looked
remarkably like the Florentine master's
gold halos,
and not understanding pain
or wanting to die for what I believe,
or what I am,
by birth.

LOVE POEM

Tree, where are your fingers?
                    They are dead.
Tree, where is the summer?
                    It has gone mad, chasing the sun.
Tree, who is the girl
with fingers like twigs?
                    She is dead.
I cannot understand her hands.
They are like twigs; and the sun,
it has died in her hair.
                    I love her and she is dead.
Tree, why are you trembling?
                    From her hands like twigs
                    and the dead sun in her hair.
I killed her, Tree;
I killed her.
                    The twigs scratched, and the sun is like
                    the dead bodies of bees twisted in her hair.
Tree, where are your fingers?
                    On her hands and in her hair.

FROM A GIRL IN A MENTAL INSTITUTION

The morning wakes me as a broken door vibrating on its
hinges.
We are drifting out to sea this morning. I
can barely feel the motion of the boat as it rocks me.
I must be a gull, sitting on the mast,
else why would I be so high above the world?
Yes.
I see everything down there—
children tucked, sleeping, into the waves,
their heads nestled in foam

                    AND I DON'T LIKE THE WAVES THEY
                    DISTINCTLY SAY THINGS
                    AGAINST ME.

The wind is blowing my feathers. How good
that feels. If the wind
had always blown my feathers, I would
never have cried
when the waves spoke
that way—
taking my brother away, when he dove in and never came
back.

                    it was because he loved the seashells
                    too much
                    i know
                    and broken water foams in my hair
                    in its new color—the color of my wing
Why don't we hear the fog-horns today?
                    IF I AM TO SIT HERE ALL DAY I MUST
                    HAVE SOMETHING TO LISTEN TO.
The waves have torn the sleeping children to bits. I
see them scattered on the crests now.
There—an arm floating by.
                    leave me alone, i have not hurt you
                    Stop pulling my wings,
                    my beak, DON'T YOU HEAR STOP IT.

There is nothing more horrible than hands
like ancient crabs, pulling at one. And they cannot
hear because they have no ears.
                    I have no ears.
I am a gull. Birds have no ears. I cannot hear
Them
or anyone.
The fingers on the dismembered arm, floating
in the waves,
can point and make signs,
but I will not hear
the waves
telling the fingers odious things about me.
I will not watch their obscenities
pointing to the bottom where the children are buried;
where he is buried;
where I am buried.

Slam the door as often as you like—you will
not wake me.
I am a gull
sitting on the mast, and I feel the ocean rocking
because I can hear nothing
but silent voices the wind carries from the past—
                    gently rocking.
The ocean is as still as a newly made bed,
rocking.

I AM AFRAID FOR THE ROSES

Girl: You have made me so beautiful
that I am afraid
for the roses.
And the bees.
Mirror: I have called nothing
I did not see.
Girl: The wind blows my hair
and whispers
'you are beautiful,'
but the trees
shake their long hair and sigh.
I will die if the sun
goes down.
Mirror: Look at me—
look, you are beautiful.
Girl: But what of the dawn?
Mirror: When you know that every shift of light
burns away your beauty
do you really fear for the roses?
cry for the bees?
Girl: You are unkind.
Mirror: I have said you are beautiful.
Do you wish any more?
Girl: What good,
if it does not last?
Mirror: Ask the roses
you cry for,
and the bees. You are beautiful
but understand so little.

VAN GOGH: BLUE PICTURE

The wind enters my room on a long thin arm.
In front of the mirror I stand,
an old woman with a green face.
My hair is on fire.
Quietly, the thin long-nailed fingers of the wind
creep over my face,
pinch off my nose with long brittle fingernails.
I am the evil witch of night,
crouching under children's beds,
making shadows in their sputtering candles.
We are friendly, the wind and I;
when you pass a sleeping town,
remember,
we may be there.
The wind winds its skinny arms about me.
Together, we walk the streets.
My hair is fire;
long tongues reach out to hold hands
with the wind.
The church spire quivers under the moon,
thinking of medieval witches who were burned near by.
I am an evil witch of the night.
The shrubbery near the church rustles.
The wind pinches off leaves with its long brittle finger-
nails.
How many people will be sleeping in the old houses
the night when my hair lets out tongues of its fire
and burns everything to the ground?

The moon is a circlet in the palm of the wind.
Someday I will slip the ring on the slender finger
of the wind and go away.

TO THE LION

I am the girl who visits the sun,
east of destiny and west of destruction,
who comes in the rain to remind you of tomorrow
and the silken trees.
I am the girl broken out of stone.
You have broken me from stone.
Lion, brush the tears from my face.

I am the girl you will never forget
because forgetting me is forgetting your own name.
It is a chain. We all love somebody else,
the lion, the sun; even the rain loves somebody
else. We know it. We know it.
We are foolish.
Lion, brush away the tears.

I am the girl, waiting for you to speak,
to open your eyes and let the words
fall out in my hands
like broken stone. I am the girl
who would not know what to do
if the words came true,
if stones tumbled in her hands.
I am the girl
who is speaking with words
and knows words will never break stone.
Lion, brush away my stone tears.

I am the girl who, for a moment, has found silence
a blessing, thankful for stone
and its confines,
and I am the girl who has broken the silence of stone
to speak
and in so doing
has sealed her voice behind fallen rocks
forever.

THE FEW SILVER SCALES

The feeling comes,
the critics say, spontaneously. A gull
swooping to the water, grabbing food, and skill,
not contrived, but gracing
the dipping wings.
I know
what they say; have never
found it so.
How stiff my wings extend,
creaking like a boat
moored,
rocking in the waves.
And how
the morsel slips away
into the water,
sliding fish—only a few silver scales in my beak
after I dive to catch it.
The feeling comes,
lurching me, and I must grab it
as best I can.
How lucky I feel
with a few silver scales
dripping from my beak.

AND THIS IS THE WAY THE WORLD ENDS: NEVER

There are ten fence posts
holding up a fence which leads
nowhere
and
on each post there is sitting a green-bird,
airing his green.
Here I come,
the destructive child,
with my glass hammer, looking
for something to strike.

       Why not a green-
       bird, suggests the little hammer,
       beginning to sing
       sharply
       with the thrill of destruction.

So,
along we go,
tapping a green-bird off each post
with a glass echo.

       Well, I said to my glass hammer,
       you can kill the birds
       but what about the green?
       Doesn't it ring in your ear
       like bells on the wind?
       Can you ever forget the green?

But already the hammer in my hand
was beginning to ring,
its glass body quivering in hopes of something to strike—
giving my knuckles tiny glass taps of reproach
for being still so long.
And the quiver of the hammer
and the guilt of my fingers,

green with commitment, balanced together
in the humming air.
Taking another look at the world
I see

> there are ten fence posts
> holding up a fence which leads
> nowhere
> and
> on each post I have just noticed a green-bird
> sitting.

COCK FIGHT UNDER THE MAGNOLIAS

Fighting cocks,
in the dark, grasp each other by the comb
and tug, energy ruffling the feathers of
old blood and new life.
One cock is struck; his eye dangles out of the socket
on a long red string.

Silent men,
in the night, stare at the spectacle, pausing
to light a cigarette, breathing tightly,
in accord with the lightning movement
of claw and beak,

Inhaling the tension of touch,
wishing the battle of the red bullets was their own
release. In despair,
we reach out, if only for the touch.
Steady hands manipulate their glowing cigarettes.

POEM TO THE MAN ON MY FIRE ESCAPE

Dark brain,
the large sponge coral,
resting in your head,
naked women flash through,
moving,
registering in the cave your fantasies—
the jewel-chest in which you plunge your arms up to the elbows
while rocks and clasps and pins gouge and graze your skin;
your bleeding
and bliss from the torn flesh.
I do not know what you were doing
or wanting to do,
climbing up the wall,
slipping on to the fire escape,
standing at the window
watching me; nor could I stop to think or
investigate. Screaming
lets it all out. Pushes your body off my eyes,
topples it off—a box of soap from the ledge—
and how or where you came from
I don't care: don't want to know.

Voyeur,
how limited your investigations become. How far
away from satisfaction.
You want to know what's inside a woman—
underneath her clothing;
you want to know more than she wants to tell?
you want to know how she is joined together,
how she bleeds,
how she creeps in your past?

You are looking in the wrong window; and I hope
you were frightened by what you saw,
I hope you know some women are dead

from the head down.
I hope you know what death on the outside
looks like
now.
I hope you saw it and were scared.
I hope you were warned that death runs all the way through.
I hope you will never forget
Fear holds us all in the palm of his hand.
The fingers fall off one by one.
The hand paralyses and drops.
Where are we when the hand drops?
Large sponge coral
sitting on top your head
dries
solidifies
is crushed finally as the earth settles
and buries us all.

COINS AND COFFINS UNDER MY BED

Three children dancing around an orange tree,
not holding hands because the tree is too round and full,
and there are only three of them:
The spiders, making their webs in the orange tree talk to the
      children.
      Do you want silver coins?
      Do you want silver cups?
      Do you remember our names?
they ask.
One little boy answers.
      I want silver rings.
      I want silver keys.
      I remember my own name. It is John.
But the spiders are making their webs larger and larger.
A yellow spider says:
      Do you hear us spinning?
      The sound
      is so loud it makes our legs vibrate.
      Do you know that David is dead
      and buried
      under this tree?
      Do you want silver coins
      to buy death away?
      Do you want silver cups to drink at your wedding?
      We spin our webs to spell our names,
      your names,
      dark names.
Three children dancing around an orange tree.
They are heavy with childhood.
      We want silver rings to link us together
      and silver keys to unlock your webs,
      and we all know our names.
      They are John.

Quietly, under the orange tree, David, who is dead and buried,
settles down.
The spiders walk over the earth like tight-rope walkers
playing above the crowd,
and I forget the coffin under my bed.

Tell me, spiders,
what I want to hear—why those children, all three of them,
sing around the tree?
They are heavy with rings.
Their bodies are made of bells,
and tell me,
what are your names, spiders?
I will write your names on coins
and throw them in the coffin under my bed.
Tell me why my hands are empty of rings yet
heaviest of all,
and my body,
like a bell, doesn't ring.
I have thousands of keys,
keys on the doorstep, in my ears,
under my pillow, in my clock,
rooms full of keys,
chests full, iron crates full.
They unlock everything,
and I hate them.
Three children around an orange tree
who know the answers to everything;
spiders who know more.
Do you see the round orange tree with three children dancing
          around it?

I am trying to believe I haven't seen, glinting through the leaves,
the hanged man,
caught by his key ring—
hanged by the key,
and the sun catching it, as he swings.

DISCREPANCIES AND APPARITIONS

This Book Is for Shepard

FOLLOW THAT STAGECOACH

The sense of disguise is a
rattlesnake and
it's easy to wake up and find it curled in your shoe.
Past Ghost Junction and Cody's Rock
the same stagecoach rattles day after day. Long days and short days
carrying the same passengers.
They keep away from you. Your six-shooter wanders into
hand, disguised
yes heavily disguised as the homosexual sheriff
bringing law and order to the West
oh but the ladies who ride that stagecoach want you to make love to
them but you never take off your shoes for fear you'll wake up only
to find a rattlesnake curled up in one of them.

Sometimes you
ride the stagecoach in another disguise.
You are in a black rubber diving suit
with your wet feet leaving prints like exotic fish on my forehead.
Under my hair is a brain
with
too many memory cells clicking off your name
trying to ascertain
your sex. I am swimming in Dry Gulch Hollow thinking of Sheriff
Stanley
who did love me but left to start the Pony Express.
His star I wear pinned to my black rubber skin-diving suit,
keeping clear of the 87 rattlesnakes swimming down the river
oh yes I catch this stagecoach you are on it Mr. Sheriff I would like
to be angry that we are not swimming in the same body of water
with every body of water suggesting so many more
the Pacific
The Atlantic
the Indian,
Arctic, Antarctic
so many oceans about, not to mention the rivers, lakes, ponds, etc.

Shall we go skin-diving I ask you but it is
clear I want to explore different areas, my own black rubber suit
showing clearly
I am a woman
why did I find you? Black Aberdeen might walk in the
ocean, or Snowfoot stroll in coral reefs
but I am looking for the most beautiful fish,
one that will shimmer his scales at me and feed me special algae,
one with spiny teeth or soft train whistles,
shiny with tamarind seeds,
metaphysical with telephone books.
Found you writing your poems on my brain with the diving fork
    and
blood covering my suit with the words,
found you trapped in Dry Gulch Hollow settling for trout,
found you and wanted to have you, willing to lock you in my jail
    with a
big iron key, wanted to say look I have found him give me the
    reward
look I have found him and he'll take me away to his territory I am
    not
afraid of rattlesnakes they sleep with me at night curled
around my warm neck we exchange poisons oh Mr. Sheriff with
    sand on
your eyes with coyotes running out of your shoulders with scorpions
in your fingers with overhand knots and loop knots and granny knots
and reef knots and bowline knots and trefoil knots and a double
    bowknot
tying your lips together and white and purple flowers on short
    stems
yes yes yes I cannot deal
with the dichotomies
would like to spend the day, day, day, day, day, day,
river day and night day, day of piranhas, and
day of old lemon seeds. wearing your black rubber suit and
    swimming
the ocean, no it's that Western body of water, Dry Gulch Hollow,

that I see you in and gives me a false sense of
your movements. Sheriff Day, the sense of disguise is
a rattlesnake. The danger is one
I would welcome
living here in this rough country
as I do
building my own house. My own disguises change so
often which one can I wear that will not frighten you though you
    are a
tough Western sheriff who obviously doesn't
frighten easily
knowing you can swim quickly away in that rubber suit.
What are you looking for? I'll show you a cemetery where you could
    find
a tombstone saying HERE LIES THE HOMOSEXUAL SHERIFF OF DRY
    GULCH COUNTY.
I didn't make this offer to the previous sheriff
oh yes you are putting on your skin-diving suit very fast running to
    the
ocean and slipping away from this girl who carries a loaded gun all
the time and keeps company with rattlesnakes and goes diving only
for the most beautiful
fish. Mr. Sheriff Day she writes you this poem from her dusty house
Walking naked is her most frequent disguise it disarms everyone
The world by now is confused with all the costumes
The world by now takes her up and tried to make her wear the right
disguises she says no no no I will go where I want when I want to
So I'll write you a love poem if I want to. I'm a Westerner and
not afraid
of my shadow.

PICTURE OF A GIRL DRAWN IN BLACK AND WHITE

A girl sits in a black room.
She is so fair
the plums have fallen off the trees outside.
Icy winds blow geese
into her hair.
The room is black,
but geese are wandering there,
breaking into her mind
and closing the room off
into its own black secret.
She is not alone, for there is the sound
of a hundred flapping wings,
and from fruit rotting in the dark earth
the smell of passing time.

A girl sits in an unreal room
combing her unreal hair.
The flapping wings of the geese have
broken plums
from the trees outside,
and the wind has frozen them all
to keep the girl in the black room
there, combing her
unreal wintry hair.

A girl sits in a picture
with the background painted solid black
and combs her hair.
She is so fair the wind has broken
plums and scattered geese.
Winter has come.
The sound of flapping wings is so loud I hear
nothing
but must only stare out of the picture
and continue combing my black
unreal hair.

ROCK

Once a rock discovered he was not a rock,
but had to go on pretending he was
because the world assumed he was
and treated him accordingly.
With his determination,
he became a successful rock.
At first he thought the burden
was an unbearable sadness.
Later, he discovered
he no longer felt
the burden.

INCIDENT OF CHERRIES AND PEACHES

When the difference is not a name,
but is more than a name,
a whole concept,
as the Milky Way is
not looking out at a band of light
but looking out,
perspective-wise,
through a sphere,
a flattish disk,

then the difference is important.
To be scrupulous about the difference,
a must.
A consistency of view,
an inch to the mile, if you will,
but consistency,
most of all,
consistency is wanted.

Simultaneity: its importance;
where the differences must be scrupulous
in order to understand the overlap.

I have told you before,
the story;
the desert.
How flat and empty.
How dry.
How a bag of oranges has dried up
and the fruit are now as husks.
How the burlap bag bumps the legs of the donkey
as we cross the desert,
and the dried oranges rattle together inside like nuts.
How I walk along through the sand, leading the donkey.
How it dries your body to a husk.
How the bag and the oranges are husks.

How no one can go through the desert
and come out with any life.
How the dried up oranges will never revive.

At the same time, I must tell you of two men.
One man is standing on a plateau.
Another man is standing on another plateau
four hundred feet higher.
The man on Plateau A feels a great gust of wind
and is blown over.
But on Plateau B there is no wind.
Plateau B is above the wind.
The man stands and enjoys the quiet.

Sometimes I also tell it this way.
One man is standing on a plateau.
Another man is standing on a plateau
four hundred feet higher.
The man on Plateau A feels a great gust of wind
and is blown over.
There is no wind below on Plateau B.
It is beneath the wind.
That man stands there and enjoys the silence.

But one way I have never told the story is this:
Eating fruit,
cherries and peaches,
I ride the donkey
in the desert.
His saddle-bags are stuffed with fruit—
oranges, peaches, grapes, cherries, bananas.
When it is night we stop on a plateau called, "Beautiful."
I lie down on the sand
which is still full of sun.
I look at the stars.
The Milky Way is to the south in the sky.
But I do not recognize most of the constellations.
The desert is very cold at night
so I wrap the old blanket around me.

I fall asleep and shiver.
I am dreaming of a gold scorpion stinging my foot
and turning my foot to gold.
In the sky the constellations move.
I am dreaming of removing a thorn from a lion's paw in the desert,
and the thorn turns gold.
In the sky the constellations shift a bit more.
I dream of a stag pawing my body to death,
and where his hooves touch my body are gold hoofprints.
The sky pictures move.
I dream of an eagle eating my fruit
and leaving gold droppings on the ground.
I dream of my fruit turning to gold
and the burlap to gold.
My donkey is gold,
and we are a clump of gold statuary lying in the desert.
When morning comes my donkey and I continue on our way
through the desert to another plateau,
but our movements are heavy
as if our bodies were covered with gold-dust
and the sand glints in the sun.
There are so many ways
of telling the story.

ICING THE TRAINS

Five hundred pound wedges of ice,
table-high,
spin down the loading-platform.
Sweating on the dock,
freezing in the icehouse,
you maneuver the blocks.
Hooked stick,
on one end a point,
catches the pieces,
whacks them in thirds,
slides them, stokes them into the chute.

Smooth and fast; caution.
Don't catch an arm or a leg,
or find it crushed off—neat as you snap a stick
for the fire.

Freight cars filled with canteloupes from California
stop in Kansas City, Mo.
for icing.
You fill them up,
and the train pulls out.
You shoot the ice down the one-half-mile dock.
You slide it into the cars.
You watch it rise in the icehouse
from the freezing level.
You split it into hunks,
and you guide it to the right places.
Don't say you don't know what I mean
when I say, "death."
I will extend your reply
"Everybody dies,"
to "Everybody dies more than once."
And ask you to recall
the simplicity and ease

44

with which you did those acts of hooking,
jabbing,
and splitting the ice,
as you moved it from house to train.
After a little practice
they were efficient,
everyday movements—
and you practiced them as well as anyone could.

FROM A GO TO B, IF YOU CAN FIND IT

I woke up
thinking I was
part of a circus act—
with you shooting
bullets around my body,
into the wall
making my outline
like a connect-the-dots game.

With a costume
I could have been anybody,
your anonymous partner,
any female in your life.
How definite you were though—
the great marksman,
whose heels left a silver streak
on the crowds,
whose hand
burned the canvas to ash,
whose voice drove in
the tent pegs with
one hammered word.

You could shoot any target;
Wild Bill was
one of your roles.
But my Annie Oakley
was an anonymous one,
rigged acts
could have as easily
made me a human cannon,
as a rifleman, a
magician, or
a trapeze star.

I threw my eyes
in the river to catch
fish for you.
I carved a tooth and put it
under my pillow for the black man.
But dozens of charms
would not change my position—
the raw materials being me.
You walked on your own fire
with bare feet.
You stood on only one
finger and tap danced against the
   wall
I remember your breath on a cold
morning—shimmering
like a goldfish, as you said,
"The wood's rotten,"
and slapped the old tree.

Yet it has stood these five years
since then and does not
seem ready to go.
Judgments are always too fast,
yet never soon enough.
You play to the crowd.
It will hurt,
desert you in the end.
These feelings we wake up with—
warnings, minute traces
of mercury in the blood.
A funny taste in the mouth.
A tooth decaying,
yet we wait until
we get a pain
in the mouth,
before we visit the dentist.

BELLY DANCER

Can these movements which move themselves
be the substance of my attraction?
Where does this thin green silk come from that covers my body?
Surely any woman wearing such fabrics
would move her body just to feel them touching every part of her.

Yet most of the women frown, or look away, or laugh stiffly.
They are afraid of these materials and these movements
in some way.
The psychologists would say they are afraid of themselves,
     somehow.
Perhaps awakening too much desire—
that their men could never satisfy?
So they keep themselves laced and buttoned and made up
in hopes that the framework will keep them stiff enough not to feel
the whole register.
In hopes that they will not have to experience that unquenchable
desire for rhythm and contact.

If a snake glided across this floor
most of them would faint or shrink away.
Yet that movement could be their own.
That smooth movement frightens them—
awakening ancestors and relatives to the tips of the arms and toes.

So my bare feet
and my thin green silks
my bells and finger cymbals
offend them—frighten their old-young bodies.
While the men simper and leer—
glad for the vicarious experience and exercise.
They do not realize how I scorn them;
or how I dance for their frightened,
unawakened, sweet
women.

ITALIAN WOMAN

If Italy is a boot,
then it is on your foot.
An elegant shoe.
Renaissance ladies,
religious and otherwise,
smile out of your face.
Your hand not forgetting a gesture.
Your mouth touching the ocean—
underneath: centuries of crushed shells,
plus the new.

MEDIEVAL TAPESTRY AND QUESTIONS

Each age brings its questions of reality:
A woman sitting alone in her tower, embroidering
all the scenes from a jousting tournament,
the red of one knight's plumes spilling over into a skein of
unused thread on her lap,
and her arms in their own grey velvet sleeves, moving swiftly,
—reflecting, as velvet will,
the shimmer of embroidered violets and coriander,
on her muslin bodice.
The hard wood of the spinning wheel in the corner.
The white sheets on her bed.
And the gallows outside her window
that cast such long shadows at twilight.
Can we question the beauty of the shadows? Their patterns
on the cobbled stones?

Perhaps there is also a question of authenticity,
looking back,
—her loneliness coming as too much of a convention,
while the maids bustle about in the great kitchen
several flights below—setting kettles over the fire,
silently pursing their pretty lips,
remembering she was once one of them,
remembering her elevation,
after the king took her to bed
and gave her fine cloths for gowns and linen,
jewels for her fingers.
And there are frowns at remembering the child in its coffin
after it died suddenly
one day.
And the reality of death is one of the questions.

Can we question the death outside the window?
How still she is all day,
her needle flashing in and out of the white cloth,

carrying all the purples and reds, greens,
violets, and yellows into stories,
finger stories,
the mind has nothing to do with.
The mind is out in the forest
—the last flick of the wolf's tail as it disappears in a thicket.
The wolf is panting as it stops running,
scenting a rabbit.
It changes its course so
as to meet
the rabbit.

But her fingers are absorbed in their own story of death
—making the thrust from the running horse
so that the red knight unhorses the yellow
and the audience applauds,
while yellow's lady fans herself,
though one would never know she feels any concern
but for her hands,
like two wild birds in their yellow gloves.
One cannot lose concern as
the colors ask the questions,
in this remote,
in this not-so-remote situation.

THE REALIZATION OF DIFFERENCE

The realization of difference comes
quietly. We are looking
at prints of Zen masters—
Chinese,
Japanese.
There is one of persimmons—
just space and persimmons.

The next was slashes of paint,
slashing trees on a slashed mountain—
two grace notes of men
climbing the white page of snow.
Your excitement,
a splatter of paint,
covered me with muddy colors.
I remembered climbing the white mountain
of ice that was your love
and feeling smaller than a grace note
on the white sheet. I remember
dying a thousand times
from the cold as I fell across the page.
I almost hated you
when, excitement rubbing off,
you said, "but,
maybe,
don't the figures stand out too much?"
A realization of difference came,
and comes and comes and comes.
When will I find a lover
who is not a blizzard of slashed feelings?
And when will the realization
of difference
come to you?

DISCREPANCIES

I

I eat the flesh off two cherries,
suck the stones,
then hold them in my hands.
They are dry,
the bones—
the answer is to leave
autobiography.

II

After two days
the white children fell down
on the desert
and begged the black ones
for milk.

But the black ones knew
where the milk was
and left it
in the refrigerator.
How long have you known
the answer?

III

When I draw the blinds
because I do not want
anyone
to know how hard
it is for me to connect things,
I leave my white hand
a jeweler's dummy
with oval nails
and a ring on the little finger
on the rim
of the shade.
You may watch the blind
for days,
the white hand cut off at the wrist
holding the blind delicately,
and never see a movement.
The photograph image being you.
I, having gone.

IV

When I talk
I want
to be
definitive.
But nothing I say
defines.
I broke the clock
thinking
how
it never skips around;
how
it always connects;
but I could not bear
it,
unrelenting,
the electric clock.

V

When I sat down
to play the guitar
I found both hands had been cut off
at the wrist.
But they were both willing to learn
to play regardless
and agreed upon instruction.
For years
I used to watch them play
when I was tired or lonely—
like two children dancing,
or skipping rope—
but they have grown up
and gone away.
Lord, how I miss them,
my hands,
my children.

VI

And when I got too lonely,
after my hands were gone,
I would watch my empty shoes
standing on the floor.
They would walk places
at night.
Sometimes all my shoes would get together
and walk off double file—
the tallest heels
going first,
the lower heels following,
the sneakers would come next,
the sandals walking delicately last.
They would go solemnly on for miles
like the penguins
you told me about,
filing into Antarctica for miles
then turning around
at some arbitrary point
and following back.
Shoes, shoes,
you have led me through many
a sleepless night.
Thank you,
Shoes.

VII

At last I saw
a needle
coming through the open
window and
I said
"I don't need a fix;
go away."
When I awaken,
black and blue prints mark
my arm
where the fingers
have held it still.

VIII

When they stumbled,
the hawks bit them on an ear.
When they stopped for breath,
the panthers growled
and nipped at their hands.
The mountain was one big diamond.
The ocean was death.
I cannot forget the sounds
they made
moaning in their sleep
at night.

IX

There is something I am trying to say
in all of this;
the raven weighs ten pounds,
and the stone eleven.
He carries the rock
and dies trying.

X

No one will understand this
even though I raise the blinds
and take away the dummy hand.
Chopping down the forest,
tree by tree,
the woodcutter does not hear
the white wolf
until it is too late.

APRICOT POEM

for Bob

Mother sits on an old wooden chair in the kitchen.
Her apron is filled with apricots.
She cuts and pits them for jam.
When the fruit cooks with sugar and pineapple, the kitchen steams
The old wooden spoon gets shiny and sticky as it stirs.
The fragrance of jam clings to my ears and fingers.

❋   ❋   ❋

Sitting
alone
my feelings turn to apricots, piled in my hands.
Their flesh;
like
it is living; yours—the apricots are feelings
in my hand.

Two kinds of jam—one for company and one for everyday.
The mixture bubbles
and the hornets hang about the back-porch screen
trying to get in.

When you are gone
I balance each fruit on the back of my fingers,
flex my hand against their soft weight.
I wait

for you. I take each apricot, separately.
I make a line of them on the wooden table.
I touch each one with a fingertip
so that
my hand is extended
palm down
and slightly cupped
to touch one apricot with each finger.

I listen for footsteps.
I look in the mirror for any sign of snow.
I remember your hand on mine,
cupping mine entirely.

I put the apricots in a bowl,
but I hold one in my hand when I go to sleep,
because of the way it feels.

Could the jam have made my cheeks soft?
It is in that kitchen of twenty years ago.
I dream and dream, waiting for you:
when you come home
I will be sleeping.
In my hands children dance;
they throw apricots for balls.

ALL GLITTER IS NOT GOLD

Dreams hold the glitter of meaning before your eyes.
The canyon, lined with grey volcanic rock,
was menacing.
But I jumped in, risking the crush,
because you were after me
and would have killed me
if you could.
Your partners were two beautiful women.

In the ocean,
there was a patch filled with spiked fishes,
and despite my fear of water
I swam
because you were waiting on the shore
with black circles around your eyes,
and I could not go back.
Dreams hold the glitter of meaning,
but is it truth seen from your eyes or mine?

I met a man on the road and he said,
"Love is that way,"
but pointed in both directions.
I said, "Which way did he go?"
and the man replied, "Neither."
In the dream I tried to find your direction,
but nobody knew. I waited,
but you did not appear. Finally,
your footsteps appeared overhead in the sky,
and I tried to get up to them.
But couldn't.

You picked stars and flung them down at me.
You said, "I feel responsible for you.
Here are some stars."
But I remembered shivering in the canyon.

I remembered swimming in the dark ocean.
You had black circles painted around your eyes,
and your stars when beautiful
were too hot to hold in my hands.
When cooled, they were rocks,
and I could not carry them; they were so heavy.

In dreams we hate and turn bitter.
Dreams hold the glitter of meaning.
Beneath our love, do we have all of these fears?

LETTER TO THE WEST

Dear _____
The wind fills the mailbox
since you have been gone
and the steel birds chatter
outside in the trees.
My house put its arms around itself
and shivers
even though spring is just around the corner.

How long have you been away? Mice
live in my teeth. The bone of my hand
forms a bird, as if to fly away.
Tomorrow I will ask the violins
that grow in my garden
if they have heard, on their strings, from you.
How can I tie the past in a bundle?
It resembles the river at flood time.
Have we no alternative to the riddles
than listening to bees in the summer?

I write to you with no address.
You could not answer—you haven't my name.
The sound of everything is chatter.
My voice changed by time
to a different speed.

ABSENCE

the hospitalman is always anxious to
get away from his
home
serving curiously
his own aims, enemies
his black bag filled with poison
    remedies
"I cannot sleep until I have saved
another life."

Part of you, an ambulance driver who prides himself
in taking the messiest calls
(head-on collisions,
scattered piece explosions)
walks with a plastic face, mustache and glasses,
    but your blue eyes

    (a thoroughbred, Kenkyusha said)

pleading the illusion,
begging release:
I am lonely.
Driving to another father's funeral,
thinking of your own father who touched you in the wrong
    places,
awakened the wrong things, the wrong feelings, at the wrong
    time,
but your face pretends not to know,
except the eyes. They tell me I'm wanted by you.

Your dream in which you were replaced by a machine,
an exquisite and delicate one,
has no room for me.
I awakened the feelings your father tried to tap,
of which you have so many,
sweet and dark as black walnuts,

hidden away in the cellar (you hope)
to dry.
No room, no room, no time, no space, no energy;
and you go to the funeral of another's father,
far away, a trip.
The mercury in my thermometer falls out in a ball
as I break everything, tearing my hands on glass;
your face comes over the phone
but it is someone else calling someone else.
Once a train rolled down the tracks and ran over her,
Anna, of the dream, her felt hat covered with deep blood
and was wet with her life after she died.

You fancy the officers' uniform, the mustache, the epaulets,
the amber mouthpiece holding the Russian cigarette,
the professional poker player's face.
And you, as a last gesture, pick up Anna's blood-soaked hat,
(dying your gloves in this motion)
kiss it, and fling it away.
The dance. We all participate in it.
You walk on stage in your brown boots, click heels,
salute the naked lady and asked her, "Madame, vas iss dis costume?"

At home, in your white orderly's jacket
you are mixing daiquiris (it's summer) for another lady. Excuse me,
she seems to be telling you, I found this blood-soaked hat outside
    your
door. Face the same. Mustache perfect. A large bloodstain
appears on the back and then comes through the front.
Excuse me, the young lady seems to be saying, I didn't mean to
    hurt you,
but I found this hat outside and the deep red stains . . .
blood on wood, you scrub and scrub; the stains endure.

A famous trip, I mean, a famous man took a trip or do I mean a man
took a trip and became famous on it or do I mean a trip became
    famous
because a certain man took it. You, you, yes, I miss you, away on
    your

famous trip. I once knew a minotaur and lived with him,
but he gave me a tail and when I turned a diamond into a dagger
we parted at blade points; does this relate? yes, this relates.

Once a man got off the train in front of my house.
once once once once once once once once. That was once.
waiting for you.
I want to tell you—I'll squeeze it all into this little space—
that I like the way you touch me. We have similar legends to offer
each other; our hieroglyphs resemble.
It is your stone I hold in my hand,
My blood-soaked hat you found at the door.

SLEEP

The mole
lifting snouts-
full of strained black dirt

        —his perfect tunnel
         sculptured
         to fit
         the fat
         body. Sleep
fits tight
—must keep bringing out.
the fine grit
to keep size
for even one day.

VIOLENCE

The wind unwinds from a silver spool
as slow as a turning mill wheel.
With stealth,
it unlooses itself in the night—
a floating bedroom curtain,
white,
beyond our sleep.

O do you know what it does?
Do you know?
The wind unwinds itself
and glides out to where the flowers are
and strangles them
in their nodding sleep.

The wind is loose,
insane,
devouring the flowers.
And do you see one floating in its mouth?

O do you know?
Do you know, Lovers,
who walk out in the morning,
what violence has been done as you slept?
And do you smell the odor of roses now,
on the breath of the wind?

MIDAS

I have learned my lesson from Midas.
I will not whisper my feelings
even to the reeds.
If I am sad the world will have to know by my thin voice.
If I am happy, they will have to believe
the moment's surface.
His donkey ears betrayed him to everyone.
If my thin voice begins to
betray me,
remember I am keeping such secrets
that even I do not know.
I must read my own signs like the pale man
who turned very pale, seeing himself
so pale
in the mirror—thinking,
I am so pale, something must be wrong.

THE OEDIPUS WITHIN

I cannot walk down the street anymore without realizing
my own death, within myself,
the slow realization of insignificance I must accept
and which will negate me,
eventually.
Is there some way to accept the truth,
to face it directly
as we would a nude statue in the museum,
without the fear we feel looking at our own unrobed bodies,
full and warm as summer lake water?
We can touch the stone breasts,
the inarticulate genitals,
and understand something about life
the curious stare at our own flesh
will not yield.
Are we afraid of our own waters
and the deep floating lilies that grow from gravelly depths?
       They will not grow from unclean water.
       Pride is our sludge.
Is there some way to look at ourselves from all sides
and realize the insignificance,
to recognize sculpture better made—
a hand carved with so much strength it could hold water,
though water cannot be held?
Is there some way to know our stone is adequate
yet not important
and still allow ourselves to be examined
and evaluated
without slipping back into the summer waters
of the lake?
Pride will not let the lilies grow.
Pride carves our eyes blind.
And if we yield to the wish that our statue be admired,
in a museum,

an incarnation of the warm, smooth waters of life into stone,
will we ruin our minds as thoroughly as if they were mauled
and chipped away by hacking chisels?
Pride carves our eyes blind.
I will never have the courage to gouge out my eyes
so that I may not be deceived by my adequacy
when I try to evaluate.
Yet,
can I realize that I,
as a statue,
am made of stone,
my eyes carved with the darkness of no sun,
and the burning lilies climb over my rigid body
flaming protest.
Everyday I walk down the street and see that I cannot see.

SCALE

Take even the jolliest person and you will find that there is a core
of sadness that he simply cannot combat. When he is left alone too
much, when he is fatigued, sometimes even when good things
happen, he simply has no choice. The sadness takes over, and he
cannot combat it.

❋   ❋   ❋

The Chinese fisherman
in the tapestry
walks
over a bridge. Snow is cover-
ing ice on the network of streams.
He cuts a hole
through
to the running water.
He baits his pole.
In one hour he will have enough to eat.

In this tapestry
the tiny figure exaggerates the size
of mountains.
Looking at it I too am overpowered
by the immensity;
yet the mountain actually
is painted only
three-fourths as high as my hand.
Losing myself thus,
the illusion being sole
measurer
and maker of sizes,
I feel you next to me—
another mountain,
though you measure only
a few inches taller
by an ordinary scale.

APPARITIONS ARE NOT SINGULAR OCCURRENCES

When I rode the zebra past your door,
wearing nothing but my diamonds, I expected to hear bells
and see your face behind the thin curtains.
But instead I saw you, a bird, wearing the mask of a bird,
with all the curtains drawn, the lights blazing,
and Death drinking cocktails with you.
In your thin hand, like the claw of a bird, because you are a bird,
the drink reflected the light from my diamonds, passing by.

Your bird's foot, like thin black threads of bone or metal staples,
has the resistance necessary to keep death at a pleasant distance,
drinking his scotch and enjoying your company,
as he seldom has a chance; the zebra hide against my bare legs
is warm. The diamonds now warm on my neck,
on my fingers,
my feet,
my ears.
How Death looks at them
and my body
and the old man desires them all.

I rode by your windows, hoping you would see me and want me,
not knowing you already had a guest.
The diamonds I put on for you,
the clothes I took off,
and my zebra—did you see his eyes just slightly narrow
as we came by?
Not knowing you would wear your bird mask,
I let you see my face.
Not knowing Death would be there,
I rode by.
And Death and I see each other now so often
I have even thought of becoming a trapeze artist so that I might
swing on the bar away from him—so far up he'd never reach me,
but instead I see him more and more with all my friends,

drinking, talking,
and always keeping his elderly eyes on me.
And you, watching me ride by on my zebra and dressed
only in my diamonds,
were my one last hope.
But even you, wearing the mask of a bird, invited him to have
a drink and left the curtains drawn for him,
sharing something you had no right to share.

THE FIRST DAY

The first day—
white wool and bumblebees.
So many flowers have bloomed
since.
You—
wrestling white panthers of sound,
I—
spinning thread.

Can you name the garments of silence we wear
to hear
bumblebees
in our names?

The first day—
dressed in stone;
and we have never spoken.

So many flowers have bloomed
since.

THE FIVE DREAMS OF JENNIFER SNOW AND HER
TESTAMENT

When the illness comes and the body
shrinks away,
becomes pale to translucence,
Death, in his black hood, comes
and stands, looking through the window.
We pull the drapes against his face:
but he waits outside.
His patience is beyond comprehension.
The girl on the bed,
pale,
also waiting, dreams.

I

She holds a mirror in her hand.
In it
there are pictures.
A lion walks towards her.
Daniel is coming from the other direction.
When they meet, they bow
and exchange presents.
Daniel gives a sword to the lion.
For its handle, there is a human skull.
The lion gives Daniel a cup
in which there is a human hand
with an embroidered cuff.
They bow to each other and walk away.
Jennifer has watched this ceremony in her mirror.
She now holds out the mirror and both Daniel and the lion stop.
They turn.
Daniel comes back and offers his cup.
But the hand in the cup moves,
grasps the mirror
and holds it up to the sun,

flashing it around
until the whole garden is set on fire.
Everything burns, but it is a quiet fire. No sounds
of crackling. No wind.
It moves up and down
like someone drawing a fire with a pencil on a piece of paper.
And Daniel is burned.
The lion. The garden.
But the cup remains intact,
the embroidered cuff immaculate,
and the sword with the human skull lies there
in the garden.

❋   ❋   ❋

Jennifer wakes for a moment.
She has a fever.
I give her water to drink.
Outside the window,
she feels the presence of Death
and falls back asleep.

II

A beautiful horse was standing outside the window.
Jennifer wanted the horse, to ride.
She looked out through her window
and saw its body,
graceful,
substantial. Whose horse
was it?
An old man came out of the brick house across the street.
A boy followed him out of the house.
He was thin and dressed in riding clothes.
The man gave him some money.
and the boy mounted the horse,
rode away. Jennifer watched him and the horse
till they were out of sight.
To lose something before you have it hurts.

A limousine, driven by a chauffeur, drew up
to the curb by the old man.
Jennifer could see
when the chauffeur got out to open the door
that he was a skeleton,
though elegantly dressed.
He held open the door for the old man,
shut it,
and got back into the driver's seat.
The limousine pulled away.

❋   ❋   ❋

I woke Jennifer for her medicine.
As I held her up,
she hardly seemed substantial enough to be sick.
What horrors can the body withstand.
She was asleep before her head touched the pillow.

III

Jennifer was swimming.
She feared the water but could not stop.
She kept going down,
farther, and farther into the lake.
A fish made out of jade and carved a thousand years ago in China
was swimming in the lake.
Jennifer saw it and was afraid.
She hated swimming.
She hated water.
She was afraid the fish would enter her mouth.
or brush against her body.
She feared death by water more than any other death.

But there was a fisherman on the lake in a boat.
He cast his net.
Jennifer and the jade fish were both entangled.
As she was drawn to the surface in the net
she saw the beautiful carvings on the jade.
She realized the fish was inanimate,
smooth and polished.

And she wasn't afraid.
It was the real fish
with real scales and gills that she feared.

*　*　*

Jennifer again awoke.
She asked me to draw the curtains,
which I did.
But Death was still there—
playing solitaire in the garden.
His black hood drawn close against the wind.
I wanted to close the drapes,
but Jennifer begged me not to.
When she fell back asleep,
I drew them.
Death I know about, but do not like to see.

IV

Jennifer dreamed that she was a harpist.
A little old man came by one day when she was sitting
in Spain playing her harp.
He sold her a monkey.
It would dance around the harp
and pluck at the strings.
She taught it to play "La Golondrina" on the harp.
and soon had it performing more difficult pieces.
She took it on a concert tour
and they made huge sums of money.
One day the monkey was offered a glass of wine
and one thing led to another.
It became an alcoholic.
It drank wine which turned into blood.
It was drinking this cup of blood that caused the monkey to die;
and Jennifer woke up crying.

*　*　*

She asked why I had drawn the curtains.
I opened them.

Death came to the window and looked in.
Jennifer sat up and looked at him.
I gave her the medicine
and she again fell asleep.

V

A spider was weaving webs
over Jennifer's mouth, ears, nose, eyes.
The spider sang this song:
>   Little Miss Muffin
>   Sat on her coffin
>   Eating her poems one day.
>   When along came a bird
>   Snatched up the words
>   And scared Miss Muffin away.

Then a bird flew over Jennifer's webbed body.
He took some of her hair for making his nest,
and whispered two words in her ear,
"diamonds," and "death."
When the bird flew away,
Jennifer woke up.
Death knocked on the door. I let him in. Jennifer spoke to him.

❊   ❊   ❊

HER TESTAMENT

There is nothing in the world I have not feared.
Everything was alive
eating me.
The shadows of real things are as destructive
as the real things themselves.
I hate them all.
both the shadows and the things they stand for.
I wanted only one thing:
the beautiful horse,
and could not have it.
A game of cards gives all the answers
but so does anything you consult.
The answer is inherent in the question.
No one really wants the answers.
My only question would be: does anyone have less fear?
And if so,
why did I have so much?

WINTER APPLES

Lady, you are walking in your sleep.
You are stealing my apples
and even though I know
you are walking
while you sleep
I cannot forgive the theft. I fear even more
what forces you out of bed;
makes you walk by
and steal apples from my bowl.

TWO SCENES FROM "THE TENUOUS CONNECTION OF DREAMS"

I believe I will look no farther.
Once when I was little,
my mother told me that if I ever found a man with a fish in his
    pocket,
a key
in his ear, and
a violin under his foot,
I should marry him.
She said, with a fish in his pocket I'd never be hungry,
a key in his ear, I'd always have a place to stay,
and a violin under his foot, I would always have music and love
(they go together).

Yesterday I met a man with all three attributes.
He said he also had a stone
for a heart and what did my mother say about that?

But I had an answer,
without even thinking.
"A rock is one thing you can always be sure of."

But he took the fish out of his pocket
and threw it in the ocean,
took the key from his ear and gave it away,
and without even looking,
stepped on the violin,
crushing it,
as he walked away.
"Lady," he said,
"I'm in a hurry," and I remembered
my mother had always said,
"Honey, beware of a man in a hurry.

One thing a woman needs
is time."

SCENE V

A Dalmatian was driving a black Chrysler down Evening Street. I
was struck by the similarity of his face to yours. So I motioned for
him to stop. When the car pulled over to the curb, and he rolled
the window down with one paw, I immediately saw that his resemblance to you was perfunctory and did not hold upon close scrutiny.

I said, "Excuse me.
I thought you were someone else."
As I said it,
the Dalmatian turned into you.
"Now I am confused," I said.
"Who are you anyway?" But you rolled up your window and drove
    away.
As the car passed me, I noticed the rear license plate.
It said, "CONFUSION."

The car was shiny black.
I had a feeling that everyone in my life at one time rode in that
    black
Chrysler as a passenger
and you chauffeured them down Evening Street or Morning Street,
or any place they chose to
go.
But you passed me just now
when the car was empty,
and I found myself saying,
"Who is this driver
that he should not know me
even when he is alone?"

INSIDE OUT

I walk the purple carpet into your eye
carrying the silver butter server
but a truck rumbles by,
                    leaving its black tire prints on my foot
and old images   the sound of banging screen doors on hot
          afternoons and a fly buzzing over the Kool-Aid spilled on
          the sink
flicker, as reflections on the metal surface.

Come in, you said,
inside your paintings, inside the blood factory, inside the
old songs that line your hands, inside
eyes that change like a snowflake every second,
inside spinach leaves holding that one piece of gravel,
inside the whiskers of a cat,
inside your old hat, and most of all inside your mouth where you
grind the pigments with your teeth, painting
with a broken bottle on the floor, and painting
with an ostrich feather on the moon that rolls out of my mouth.

You cannot let me walk inside you too long inside
the veins where my small feet touch
bottom.
You must reach inside and pull me
like a silver bullet
from your arm.

THE MAN WHO PAINTS MOUNTAINS

You are cut off
like the Chinese hermit. You think of the snowy mountain,
look at your hand holding its cup of tea
and see the impossible comparison.
How can a word bring you close—
one brush stroke after another: the Tao does not give
everyman the same idea
of mountain.
Your brush stroke, with skill, glides into mountain
but will anyone ever know what you mean by it?

You are cut off
like the Chinese hermit. Each brush stroke gets smaller,
more precise:
but you have given up all hope of communication
and scarcely speak.
Mountain after mountain
fills your work. And they say, "Oh, yes,
he is the man who paints mountains."

DEATH AND THE MISER

Skinny-bones, Death,
your old foot coming through the door,
your body
as frail as china teacups
    (brittle
    bone china);
from my bed, my old age,
I welcome you.

This room is small,
can hardly accommodate the two of us.
Yet all of my selves,
younger,
even newly-born,
are present. And my body has shrunk—
takes up less space
than I remembered.

As a baby I had a bag of gold coins to
count,
to chew,
to build
and throw. My building blocks
and my toys were money.
As a young man,
I exchanged every juice I had in my body for coins,
and my skin grew old and yellow
in the reflection of these coins.
I see my middle-aged self rummaging in my chest,
and small animals steal away the money,
coin by coin.
The anxiety it causes
is like seeing a beautiful woman, your wife, say,
being stolen in bits from all sides
by young men who flatter her

and take her beauty
bit by bit.
So my money goes—yet I have so much I can never
lose it all.
But these pinchings hurt.
I hear the moneybags sigh as they sink a little
each time they lose a coin.

No, these things have gone before.
Now, I welcome Death,
the old skinny-bones, as he genteel-
ly nudges his cane through the door.
My encounters with life have been hard
and metallic.
Though my purses are full,
my body is like empty money-sacks, just as glad to be folded and
    put away.
But even in death I will not lose
because I will have two coins placed firmly over my eyes.

A CHILD, A WASP, AND AN APRICOT TREE

What is there we do not know about death
that cannot be pulled out of our mouths
like a long white ribbon, stretching
and stretching
out
beyond our own senses?
A bird pulling a worm out of the ground.
It is burrowed there inside,
living alone in the dark.

Here, let me draw a picture for you.

I have drawn a stick figure of a child. And
here is a wasp,

perhaps a little out of proportion with the figure
but imagine that if the child is child-size,
the wasp is wasp-size.

Now, here is a flower.

The child picks the flower
which happens to be an apricot blossom.
But, as you might suspect,
the wasp is in the flower.
When the child puts his face to the blossom to smell it
he notices the wasp.
His mouth opens in surprise, and his eyes get large.
But it is too late.
The wasp has caught the white ribbon of fear
out of the child's mouth
and, buzzing loud,
he pulls it out, longer and longer,
and winds it around the child—winds and winds

until the child is wrapped in white ribbon
from head to toe,
bound in white strips, as a mummy,
and the ribbon breaks off in the constricted mouth.
When the wasp, of our picture,
flies away, he flies pulling the ribbon,
but instead of pulling it tighter about the child,
he sets it in opposite motion,
spinning the child around without control
as the farther the wasp flies
attached to the ribbon,
the faster the child spins, but the more the tape unwinds
from him,
until at last he is free,
and dizzily he sees the white ribbon vanishing
beyond the apricot tree with the wasp.

I do not mean to say that the child is thinner
for losing great lengths of his white tape
or to imply how much he has inside
   —perhaps he, himself, is made of tape—
but only to draw a picture of a child, a wasp, and
a blossoming apricot tree
which are in themselves too lovely
to allow much thought of death.
It is behind their masks
I hide my own fear.

THE PRIESTESS NO. 1

Very long ago,
very specifically,
very instrumentally,
very much in keeping with her hungers and fears,
a woman fanned the evening fire
and said
that her purity was her undoing.
The fire rose under the kettle and burned her meal.
The fire in her body rose
and burned her arm and thigh.

I have found, taking the burned pieces out of my stew,
that something similar was true here.

Lord,
My Lord,
how I worshiped you.
How I gave every breath
whether cinnamon or garlic
And how I was burned across pelvis
and chest
knee
shoulder
tongue.

This fire I make now
is a fire
with a different wood
—yes, and in a different grate.
And if you look closely
at its colors
you will see the woman-eyed chameleon.

This fire will be
so beautiful
when it burns.

A POEM FOR THE YAM FESTIVAL

Your hand
A mountain range un-
Measured.
   You Ask Me:
   Are Mountains Your
   Measure And, Yes,

Yes. the
Answer is a
Measure.

Yes. the
Answer is a
Mountain range unmeasured.

WIND SECRETS

I like the wind
with its puffed cheeks and closed eyes.
Nice wind.
I like its gentle sounds
and fierce bites.
When I was little
I used to sit by the black, potbellied stove and stare
at a spot on the ceiling,
while the wind breathed and blew
outside.
"Nice wind,"
I murmured to myself.

I would ask mother when she kneeled to tie my shoes
what the wind said.

Mother knew.

And the wind whistled and roared outside
while the coals opened their eyes in anger
at me.
I would hear mother crying under the wind.
"Nice wind," I said,
But my heart leapt like a darting fish.
I remember the wind better than any sound.
It was the first thing I heard
with blazing ears,
a sound that didn't murmur and coo,
and the sounds wrapped round my head
and huffed open my eyes.
It was the first thing I heard
besides my father beating my mother.
The sounds slashed at my ears like scissors.
Nice wind.

The wind blows
while the glowing coals from the stove look at me
with angry eyes.
Nice wind.
Nice wind.
Oh, close your eyes.
There was nothing I could do.

BEYOND ALL SENSE OF TIME

I am a most rational man, but in my dreams
I wear a mask, curtaining myself . . .
I ride a green horse, and diamonds
shower down from his ears,
glitter raining down on the road
and vanishing like bubbles when they touch the ground.
A child with yellow hair stands
in the road and as my green horse goes,
we stop beside his smiling face,
and diamonds tumble over him.
Diamonds fall, as skyrocket sparks
shattering down—oh, the stars,
the rocky stars cover the child,
bury him. My green horse neighs
and moves along. Backwards
I stare, at the road—the heap of diamonds sparkling
on the dirt, burying the child,
dead, with yellow hair;
And green hoofprints mark the road
as I ride on. A green horse
with diamonds in his ears carries me
up the road and if I did not wake,
green hooves would carry me
beyond all sense of time.

ORDINARY POEM

"Where does the rain come from?
Oceans are the chief sources of rain
but lakes and other sources of water also contribute to it.
The heat of the sun evaporates water into the atmosphere.
There it remains as invisible vapor until it is con-
densed, first into clouds, and then into raindrops.
This happens
when the air is cooled (*see* Clouds; evaporation; water)."

Compton's Pictured Encyclopedia
Vol. 12, p. 88.

Where does the sun come from?
You are the chief source of sun,
but when you are not around, thinking of you contributes to it.
If I were metaphysical
I could say that everything revolves around you
and that makes a system
but I am not metaphysical.

Where do you come from?
You come from history, as everyone
comes from history.
This happens
when the air is cooled (*see* History; evolution; man) and
rain is made
which comes from the sun
which is all of us
because we live for the sun.

When it is raining
we feel drops
sometimes.
Sometimes
we feel larger masses.
Sometimes we feel rain when it is raining
and sometimes we feel

lots of water
which we know is rain
but feels more like water
than rain.

When the sun is shining
we feel warm.
Sometimes we feel warmer.
Then we feel hot.
When we get very hot,
we start feeling wet.
This is not the wet feeling of rain
or even of larger masses of water.
This is the wet feeling of heat.
Thus heat
hotness
of sun
could be said to produce a certain feeling of water.
Thus when the sun shines,
we feel warm,
then hot,
then water.

Where does this water come from?
Oceans are a chief source of rain.
But this water we have already
said
is not rain.
Rain is in drops,
cool.
Rain is ordinary
The sun is ordinary.
You are ordinary.
At least
as ordinary as the rain or the sun
But I don't think you are ordinary
like
this writing is

or poems
or the forms everything takes.
Even my love for you is ordinary—
at least as ordinary as
rain or the sun.
That is what I like best about
it.
I love you very much because you are not ordinary.

Where does love come from?
Oceans are the chief source of rain
but lakes and other sources of water also contribute to it.
The heat of the sun evaporates rain into the atmosphere.
There it remains as invisible vapor until it is con-
densed, first into clouds, and then into raindrops.
This happens
when the air is cooled.

All of this about rain and sun should relate
to love
because they are all so ordinary
and it is ordinary for poets
to make comparisons like this.
But if you do not find relationships,
that is ordinary too.
Since, the sun is the sun.
Rain is rain.
And they all mean whatever they mean.
                              The end.

TENDENCIES WE HAVE ALREADY SEEN

I. DANCERS

Entering naked

in your toe-shoes,
you say you'll take everything away
except your own exquisite
self.
Yet your Japanese face,
your Italian breasts,
your Swedish shoulders,
and your Indian feet
all pull in different directions.
A multiracial audience applauds you;
the Japanese like your face.
The Italians your breasts.
The Swedish your shoulders.
And the Indians your feet.
But each would cut off his portion
and throw away the rest.
Thus your naked body
fights with itself
not knowing which factions to please.

II. SCULPTORS

You model a man with a tiny head
and an enormous penis
You worry about space and image.
You drink a lot
and please the women.
Do you model from life:
for instance, is your own head small and your penis large?
Or are these relations a morality,
saying, thus things should be in life.
Or, is it all an abstraction.

Nothing you deal with.
That big cock just being something good to hold on to
while you're meticulously working
on details of the tiny head?

III. MUSICIANS

Neptune, an old man, blows his pitchpipe
and your ear catches every sound.
If sounds were a bag of mixed spices,
you could sort them out with many sieves.
If melody were a grey thread
mixed in with a thousand other varied threads,
you could pick it out with your eye.
So, when you strike an enormous gong,
and everyone gasps at the overwhelming
powerful sound,
you stand listening
rapt,
but not at the grandeur.
Rather, you are hearing
the overtones,
the small pitches that change.
You can analyze the whistle of a bird
or the wind
blowing through a broken pane of glass.

IV. POETS

You visit an old witch on the outskirts of town.
She gives you the moon
to put in a satchel.
She tells you how to shake it
(like a coconut)
and where to put it when.
You ask her how many moons
she has already given out,
and she shakes her head. Not more than there are in
the sky.

Saturn has moons, and Jupiter has moons
and maybe many others.
So you take your bulging satchel home,
and you do everything she says.
But in the city there are five hundred
other new moons
being shaken and held
and others,
old ones dried up into mothballs
with age.
The moon in your satchel is fresh fruit.
Eat it now,
and buy another tomorrow.
Make the old witch
rich.

THE HELMS BAKERY MAN

The Helmsman came in a yellow truck,
with a hard-shelled top, like a beetle.
Sometimes when I am in bed at night,
I remember his donuts and fresh bread,
white-sacked,
sliding out in the smooth wooden tray.

I sleep under a quilt patched with roses and signs of the zodiac.
Nine swords hang over my bed.
In the chest beneath me
are bones.
Each sword has cut some part of me,
and I cling to the sword,
keeping close the memory of an eye or an arm
or a heart.

Sometimes I wake up at night.
Saturn glows like a ruby.
Outside,
Around me,
it is dark,
but I hear the flutter of enormous wings.
It is a hard life,
with bones under you
and swords over your head.
But it is everyone's life.
At night under the blanket of the zodiac
I hear a little toot,
see the yellow truck come down my old street;
and there is the Helmsman,
asking what I want today, as I hand him my nickel.
"A bun," I say.
And he gives me one with the moon
in white icing decorating the top.

THE PIANO

The Piano
all strings contained,
remains silent,
until someone
plays.

The obvious.
As when a white jade animal falls you are
    aware of its substance.
It rattles
on the floor.

But the obvious piano is not always played.
Three more analogies are implied.
Love, the poem,
exploits them.

POSSESSION POEM

This is my world. You can't
come in.
This is a list of things in my world.   oranges You can't
have them   mirrors
I will tell you a story about each   birds
but it is meant to lead you only so far   children
and no farther.   horses
If you open the last door at the end of   metal
the hall,
you will find all the wrong things—Remember
Bluebeard's wife
and the room full of bodies.
When you open the door remember
they all died different deaths
and none was happy for having found the door.
Remember to go only as far as you have the key.

I. ORANGES

There was one orange on the tree
and you walked by.
How could you know that
Death lived inside,
sleeping in the membranes.
How could you know
he would unfold,
wearing pointed slippers,
velvet doublet,
and a gold cod-piece
the moment you opened the orange.
How could you have known
he would step out and kill you?

Remember the orange
shining on the tree
alone—

and remember not to touch
if there is only one.

My hand holds the orange.
Your hand holds mine.
Remember, we hold death
in our hands and
it is because we hold
what is not our own—
that death is inside
and we hold him.

II. MIRRORS

Opposite the orange tree
is a lake.
The lake is filled with mirror fish.
You throw in your net
and hundreds of mirror slivers are hurled up,
swarming and glinting.
When you eat a mirror fish
you die, let me tell you,
when you are bored with this world,
the mirror is the answer.
It reflects everything
and in reflecting
shows the changes. For instance,
you have changed
since I met you.
I must have changed too.
What has happened? I hold mirror fish
moving anxiously in my grasp
and you take my hand.
What are you doing?
The lake is full of fish.
I have only a few in my hand.
Surely you mistake the situation for another.
You see my changing face,

reflected in these mirrors
and mistake it for something in your past.
Do not trust the mirror.
It leads from boredom
to death. What are you doing with my hand.
Surely you mistake me for someone else.
It is the deception of mirrors.

III. BIRDS

Over the lake
a bird flies.
It is named, "Silence."
Watch its flight over the lake filled with mirror fish.
Only this bird has as many disguises as we can invent.
Only this bird
is my children,
flying away,
a figure that comes and goes,
mainly a dark shadow,
always slightly over my head,
—sometimes in my dreams at night.
It is a bird and nothing more.

IV. CHILDREN

When I cannot talk about something,
I have several alternatives.
I can say nothing and risk being dull
or say too much and be even duller.
Sitting alone, I think of my conflicts.
How I want to be a child
but how unhappy childhood is.
You, who speak of father with his gold watch, cigars, and whiskers
remembering the trips, and the holidays from school,
are nostalgic for something I never saw.
Can I even remember my father,
and certainly he was not nice,
if I do remember him.

What trips we took were sad or horrible
the nightmare of childhood
is a broken nag,
too pitiful to be despised;
Put it out to pasture,
or better,
shoot it—why waste the space?
It was a broken horse
before I ever had it.
Can I reminisce for beauty I never saw?
Can I long for something beautiful
when I know it is really ugly?
How can I talk,
say anything,
when the conflict gets too strong?

V. HORSES

All right, Daniel,
I'm tired of talking to you in symbols.
Let us use plain language,
hard facts,
Let's get this out in the open,
make it real.
I was in this chair first.
That means it was mine first.
When I got up for a glass of brandy,
I did not think you would immediately
sit down
in my chair.
I know about the nine points of possession
and would like to inform you
that what you are doing may be legal,
but it's immoral.
I, myself,
am always on the other side of the fence;
but maybe both sides are the same.

Anyway,
if you don't get up out of my chair,
I'm going to be mad, just plain angry.
I'll never speak to you again.
I'll tell your friends what You're really like.
I'll even leave you if you don't get out of my chair
—and then you'll be sorry.

Oh please,
won't you get out of my chair.

VI. METAL

When I got up from that chair,
you sat down in it.
Please don't think I didn't realize the world was turning
to metal.
However,
it was this last prerogative of movement
I appreciated
and wanted
and which allowed me to leave
what was mine.
I anticipated the coming transformation
of all things to metal,
could already feel the nails
pounding iron plates over my brain and eyes.
When we die, we turn to metal;
when we live, our lives become
gradually cast over with a metal film.
The robot is a joyful alternative,
being born out of metal
and never experiencing
the change.
If I ever had one complaint in this world,
it is that my mechanism
was not quite perfect;
that, as a machine,
I was almost a total failure.

THE GEORGE WASHINGTON POEMS

To My Father & My Husband

GEORGE WASHINGTON AND THE LOSS OF HIS TEETH

the ultimate
in the un-Romantic:
false teeth

> This room became a room where your heaviness
> and my heaviness came together,
> an overlay of flower petals once new and fresh
> pasted together queerly, as for some lady's hat,
> and finally false and stiff, love fearing
> to lose itself, locks and keys become inevitable.

The truth is that George cut down his father's cherry tree,
his ax making chips of wood so sweet with sap they could be
sucked, and he stripped the bark like old bandages
from the tree for kindling.
In this tree he defied his dead father,
the man who could not give him an education and left him to
suffer the ranting of Adams and others,
those fat sap-cheeked men who said George did not know enough
to be president. He chopped that tree—
it was no small one—down and the dry leaves rustled
like the feet of cows on grass.
It was then that George lost his teeth. He
fell asleep next to his pile of kindling wood and dreamed
the old father came chasing him with a large penis swung over his
shoulder. But George filled his mouth with cherries
and swallowed the bleeding flesh
and spit out the stones in a terrible torrent at his father.
With the pits of the
cherries
came all of George's teeth,
pointed weapons to hurl from the mouth at his father,
the owner of that false cherry tree.

We all come to such battles with our own flesh,
spitting out more than we have swallowed,
thus losing part of ourselves.

You came to me thus
with weapons

        and this room is strewn with dead flowers
        that grew out of my breasts and dropped off
        black and weak.
        This room is gravelled with stones I dropped
        from my womb, ossified in my own body
        from your rocky white quartz sperm.
        This room is built from the lumber of my thigh,
        and it is heavy with hate.

George had a set of false teeth
made from the cherry wood. But it was his father's tree
His lips closed painfully over the stiff set.
There is no question,
either,
where you
got the teeth in your mouth.

GEORGE WASHINGTON AND THE DREAM OF GLADYS HINDMARCH

The dream takes four shapes, she said.
And it was apparent that her dream was classical.

I. The Shape of Voicelessness

of
to
under
around
through
with
against
about
Wandering in the corridors of the castle with a 3 foot whiskey
bottle he found all the floors were escalators
moving
under his feet.
"Looking for the object. Looking for the object," on
each shoe
a small mole crept announcing the meaning.
We all run down the corridors at night
screaming
but the form voicelessness takes in our sleep
is to make us call names
that we know
will never answer.

II. The Shape of Sightlessness

George, you had been turned naked and ragged
not into the snow at Appomattox
but into the delightful summer of Martha's Vineyard.

Two ladies lay in ruffled bikinis on the beach
lapping
up sun.

"Fuck you, fuck you," they cried as they saw
you approaching naked but paradoxically
ragged
not conforming to the standards of their beach.
You,
in fact,
blanched in shame,
your stiff Aquarian face longing for the proprieties of uniform
—hating the raggedness enforced upon you.

You have told me, George Washington, in long letters
your painful memories of this scene,
how upon seeing their bodies you immediately
had an erection
and they tittered at your condition,
and how through it all you felt mainly ragged
because they saw you thus
until even your penis felt ragged
and you wanted to tell these sleek tall beauties you weren't
always this way.
George, you should have thrown the mermaids into the sea.
You and they—natural visions,
contiguous events we all impose upon one another.

III. The Shape of Hearinglessness

The moon obviously resided in her face.
The tissues were obviously saturated with milk.
The feeling of polished stone established itself against her ears,
and her cheek was rewound with metal tape.
Living in the caves of her throat were pictures, not words.
Her hand found clay to squeeze into bowls.
An object as white and soft as pork.
An object as silent as pillows.
She was as still as wet paper.
The moon obviously resided in her face.
And walked noiselessly to the sky each night.

IV. The Shape, Syncopes; Synapses

On your horse, George Washington,
a chestnut,
Gladys rode behind you, the saddle bags
stuffed with torn hundred dollar bills,
each of which you had only half.
As there was no map, she
drew one on the back of your shirt.
You picked up peanut butter sandwiches from the settlers
along the way,
but this was a business trip and required very little
eating.
Going to the Federal Reserve Deposit you had
told her
to turn in the defaced money.
This you had told her and disappeared.

Man is a linear object.
In terms of time his goals are simple.
Each dream presents one image.
We hold it
as a pipe
or an apple
or a wrench to be used at the sink.

GEORGE WASHINGTON SLEPT HERE

Scattered
in the barnyard
fading into the stained color of old bureau drawers
bones from many
dismembered chickens
lay
almost concealed by the barnyard dust.
The place, transformed
by its new owners,
had lost the tumbledown look of a chicken farm. It was in fact
the home of the retired
president
of our country. No. 1 Uno. The first.
ola, or u, whatever word ending would indicate
specialness.
He came for a southern fried chicken dinner
and mint juleps. He fell asleep in the swing and he stayed. They
put his name on the door and said Washington
slept here.

> Here in this place
> you and I slept. We dreamed
> in unison
> of the grey battleships
> They came secretly into the harbor
> and in fatigues you watched them lining up
> cannons, missiles, the accoutrements
> of war.
> But a pair of red shoes
> stained red from a gaping hole in my arm
> was sitting on deck
> tiny, pointed, high-heeled,
> and the gunners could not miss them,
> threw them
> overboard.

With one arm around me
in love,
devotion,
the other was smashing the back of my head with
a rock.
Man in the grey uniform,
man that I still love,
man who makes me weep in the stomach as I walk
calmly thru the world,
we slept together long enough to be joined at
the thigh bone,
and the dream offers no hope
with the ocean turning to blood from those
stained abandoned shoes.

The open declarations of love
must turn on themselves,
must attack me,
must tattoo my mouth with pain.
I am afraid of talk,
having once said
"I love you," and not wanting to repeat
such a mistake.

George Washington slept here
in this very bed. They put on clean white sheets
for him
and a warming pan into the
iron-cold bed.
An interest in history divulged the maker
of the bed—
one A. Johnson Peabody by name, old carver of wood,
designer of simple sturdy frames.
History will also tell you the date,
1794,
a year when the music box came over from France
and one new harmonium.
The chairs made in this new colony
were more beautiful than high court furniture of Louis Quinze.

Oh Washington,
you slept here,
you left the imprint of your tired head
in the goosey pillow.
My own historical bed is empty without you,
father of my country.
Your eagle
appears in the night to pull out all my hidden currency
from drawers and closets
and then flaps over my narrow bed once.
I dream of you just vaguely
sailing on the Mediterranean with a black-headed woman
whose hair is filled with snakes,
dancing in Sweden with a black-haired woman whose belly is
filled with ice,
bicycling in Germany with the black-headed woman whose eyes are
melted lead.
You travel with her away from your country, your history,
and I sit by the fire in winter
chatting with
Betsy Ross
as she sews me a new dress
made from the American flag.
George Washington slept here is written
over the fireplace
but the fire burns now
without any of the wood from his historic
cherry tree.

GEORGE WASHINGTON

Wearing a green silk dress
I drove to California with a giraffe who looked like George
　　Washington.
The roads were long
and covered with ivory boxes.
We stopped at a filling station for gas and found that the next
hundred miles of road would be dangerous.

I left notes for you in every ivory box we passed.
The gold clasps did not open
properly.
I wrote letters to you
and fastened them with gold clasps.

But my green dress wore out long before I reached California.
The giraffe abandoned me at the first zoo.
I kept calling INFORMATION and asking for George Washington,
but his phone service had been shut off
in Washington. New York. LA. and
Palm Beach.

"We can connect you with the new president," said the operator.
"It won't do any good," I answered.
"I must reach George Washington. No one else will do."

So I left more notes for you in the ivory boxes.
I kept saying, "Let me know where you are."
I travelled all the roads in the country.
I left notes everywhere.
I sent you letters with gold catches unclasped.
I telephoned every place I could think of.
My giraffe left me after finding a zoo.
My green silk dress wore out.
I have no clothes.
Please tell me
what I am doing—riding over the same dangerous 100 miles

everyday,
leaving letters in ivory boxes.
They all bear your name.
Please tell me what I'm doing?
Why?
Sometimes I do remember reading in the paper over 200 years ago
that you died—I must know
you're dead
by now.
Please tell me what I'm doing,
George Washington.
Please tell me what I'm doing,
—for my own good.

WAITING UNDER GEORGE WASHINGTON'S BRIDGE

The smoke pours from the chimney—a bear
with curved claws walking into the sky.
My sadness comes from having too much happiness thrust on me,
and my incomplete acceptance
of the bad with the good.

I walk down the street—a bear lumbers beside me.
We walk to the river to meet George Washington under his bridge.
I have been too severe, he says in a letter from California,
and he wants to talk to me about psychology.

Under the bridge, the bear and I sit down,
water lapping at our feet.
I wait.
The sun shines on the bear's fur and makes him warm.
It doesn't touch me at all.
My sneakers are wet.
I am cold. It gets dark and
George Washington still doesn't come.

It is such scenes I think about when you leave me alone—
of George Washington's never coming back.
Sitting under the bridge,
waiting all night. Then the bridge lights up.
American flags are hung all over.
A band plays, "The Stars and Stripes Forever,"
and George's boat comes in.
He stands and waves to the crowd.
"George Washington,
George Washington,
here I am," I shout. He smiles,
waves,
passes by.
"I had an appointment with him," I say to
everyone around me,
but they give each other knowing looks.

"You're too young to have an appointment with the president,"
they say; and I tell them he wanted to talk to me about psychology.
But the band plays
and he floats by once more
and everyone continues to wave.

What am I doing here
under the George Washington Bridge?
You left me for no reason
than that you tired of my company;
I thought it didn't matter,
but now I find
it does.
And I wonder what
am I doing here;
so I write George Washington another
letter.

EXPOSITION IS THE HARD PART—THE REST FOLLOWS

five rooms at least, in this house.
No furniture
except a fallen bureau.
I have a feeling it is a new house—quiet and bright.
This is the house where I thought I would find George Washington,
but no sight of him as I stepped through the doorway.
I feel threatened from you
so I seek my friend George Washington,
but no sight of him as I stepped through the doorway.
He has often written me inspiring letters. His last
contained a postscript:
"beware of the 19th".

Because I am hysterical
I make a trip to this house to find out
what can help me,
for I am afraid of all things
and during the last few days have been feeling depressed.
This house is strange.
It is full of animals:
a badger hanging from the ceiling,
a wolf with a fat white chest standing on the fallen bureau,
a mouse and an armadillo nibble on the floor.
The place is a wonder of animals with an ocelot,
a cat,
a white bear,
a bat,
an animal with zebra stripes and elk horns,
a swallow,
a butterfly,
a wild duck,
a dog,
and three birds I cannot identify
all wandering in these rooms.
A girl with no clothes on stands in one empty room.

"George Washington," I call.
No one answers.
"Hello," I yell out again.
The animals seem to be stuffed
in their positions—they do not move
and they do not frighten me.
One of the birds has a note in his beak.
I reach up on tiptoe and pick out the slip of paper.
It says, "You were foolish to come.
There is nothing here but an empty house,"
It was signed, "George W."

I saw George Washington's portrait on the wall.
He looked like he was floating on clouds.
"George Washington," I said to the portrait, "give me some advice."
Just then he came in the door,
stamping mud off his shoes. Behind him were
dozens of animals and a life-sized wooden statue of a woman with
the name MARTHA
on a band across her shoulder
and under the arm.

George Washington asks me why I am here
at his house.
I tell him I am lonely
and was frightened when I got his message.
He asks me what I was afraid of,
and I tell him my fears:

Every night when I get ready to go to bed,
there is a hand, limp,
detached from the body
lying under my pillow. It holds a note from you.
I open it in fear.
It says you will not come back,
And I slip the note back into the lifeless hand
trying to pretend I haven't read it.

George Washington leads his animals in a chorus from "The Star
Spangled Banner"
and they all march out.
I see a hand lying on the floor by the door.
It has a note in it.
I refuse to pick it up.
The story could repeat itself time and again.
Perhaps the man on the Quaker Oats box is George Washington.
Perhaps the house full of animals is the only place to go.
Exposition is the hard part—the rest follows:
just describing the limpness
and pale color
of the hand as it lies under my pillow waiting for me
with the message I fear
as much as death.

GEORGE WASHINGTON AND THE PEARL NECKLACE

History informs us of
civility.
Thus I could sit with you in my drawing room
while eagles flew around my head,
circling
waiting for the juicy red heart to
fall out in the canyon at my feet. Could
love be more arbitrary?
If you said you
wanted me
tomorrow,
I would come.
But in lieu of such a declaration
my body itself
develops the
hawk head.
In secret I go to my chest and look at the jewels
you once gave me,
wondering why the lapis and obsidian and amber
do not substitute for you,
so much more real,
substantial
and lasting they are.

            One morning George Washington woke up
            only to find his shoe,
            the left one,
            filled with pearls, rolling under his arch, when he
            slipped on the shoe to see if they might disappear.
            But the pearls
            were milky enough
            to fill his mouth
            and he thought of Betsy Fauntleroy,
            the girl he loved in his
            20th year.

Pouring the pearls out of his shoe he had them
strung by his valet
and he sent them in a parcel
to Betsy,
now 40 and fat.
Naturally
she returned them at once,
not feeling such a gift was appropriate,
but her heart was giving trickles of blood
at George's long memory.

In hawk-headed silence
I watched your long memory tying itself in coils,
telling me it was shortened
and there was nothing between us. The canyon
at my feet too wide
for any rope to be thrown across.

George, the pearls rolling in your shoe
one morning, somehow cover
my feet when I sleep.
The dream recurs,
of walking and the ground's covered with pearls,
slipping under my feet,
upsetting my balance. I reach for them and they
vanish like bubbles. Yet those jewels
are in my chest each morning,
thick chunks of rock
reminding
of other times,
other conditions.
The pearl necklace, George, a classical gift you
wished to give
and other historical considerations
standing in the way,
other images to occupy your mind.

GEORGE WASHINGTON MEETS BAUDELAIRE

The warning was subtle,
the sound of a harpsichord tinkling in his ear
when he knew there was no
instrument around.

"All my life I have been afraid of anachronisms."
George said this
looking at his Bulova wristwatch,
and at that moment Baudelaire drove up in his Ford Car.
Now if you have never seen Baudelaire in
his Ford Car
it is a sight you should be informed of,
his white hair hanging to his shoulders,
goggles and duster covering a stooped old man,
and on his shoulder sits a lynx
while he periodically holds up a pitch pipe
and blows middle C.

When you meet Baudelaire
you should have something special to say,
Baudelaire was a man of words

I met Baudelaire once
and he gave me the key he used for tuning the piano.
"Always get middle C first,"
were his instructions.
With that sound in your ear
all scales are adjustable.

I have only learned to play one piece
but that is sufficient for tuning pianos—
    the minuet I once saw George dance.

Holding me close,
the warning was subtle,
the sound of a harpsichord tinkling in my ear
when I knew there was
no instrument around.

GEORGE WASHINGTON AND THE INVENTION OF
DYNAMITE

Since the invention of dynamite, George,
you have been a different person.
Wearing your wool scarf and standing near the river's edge
with an icy wind coming off it
you meditate.
We all
know the story of the famous discovery,
the inventor's guilt
and humanitarian needs,
but we do not
know
of the care which weighs you,
the thoughts of your own effort night after night
working out formulas for the power and then just as you were
ready to reveal it,
another man
presenting it to the world with his noble sentiments
high wishes
and of course his guilt.

But George, as you walk alone by the river
or sip your midnight cognac with the other bachelors
or are at your desk drafting a new bill, remember
that you have had the honor of being our first president
and are alive today
several hundred years later
and that is no small accomplishment. George,
sometimes I mistake the powder from your wig for dust
or your voice is like two stations on the radio
and I cannot see you as you sit down quietly beside my bed. You
are different since this
crazy invention
and I wish I could restore you to your
original polite calm.

Even your portrait agitates
and I see it slightly move on the wall
with your sigh—

No wonder, George,
you are such a tight-lipped man.

PATRIOTIC POEM

George Washington, your name is on my lips.
You had a lot of slaves.
I don't like the idea of slaves. I know I am
a slave to
too many masters, already
a red cardinal flies out of the pine tree in my eye swooping
down to crack a nut and the bird feeds on a tray draped with
a thirteen-starred flag. Underneath my heart where the fat clings
like bits of wool
I want to feel a man slipping his hand inside my body
massaging the heart, bathing
it in stripes, streams of new blood with stars floating in it
must pass through my arteries, each star pricking
the walls of veins with the prickly sensation of life.
The blood is old,
perhaps was shipped from Mt. Vernon
which was once a blood factory.
Mr. Washington, the pseudo aristocrat with two large fish instead of
feet, slapping around the plantation,
managing the country with surveyor's tools,
writing documents with sweet potatoes, yams, ham hocks, and
    black-eyed peas,
oh I hate southern gentlemen, too bad he was one;
somehow I've always hated the men who ran my country
but I was a loyal citizen. "Take me to your leader,"
and I'll give him a transfusion of my AB negative blood with stars
floating in it. I often said this
in a spirit of devotion, chavinistic passion,
pining secretly for the beautiful Alexander Hamilton but making do
    with George who, after all, was the first president
and I need those firsts. On my wall, yes the wall of my stomach;
on my money, yes play money and real money, money I spend and
    money

I save, in and out of pocket; on documents, and deeds, statuary,
   monu-
ments, books, pictures, trains, old houses, whiskey bottles, and even
sewing machine shuttles there is his name
and my commitment, after all, is to names, how else, to what else
do we commit ourselves but names
and George I have commited myself to you. No Western sheriffs
   for me;
they only really like men and horses and sometimes gun play.
I guess I'm stuck with you, George, despite your absolute inability
to feel anything personal, or communicate it,
or at least share it with me.
Thank you at least for being first in your white linen and black coat.
My body, the old story, is my country, the only territory I control
and it certainly has been torn by wars. I'd like to think the
Revolution is over and that at last I am going to have my first pres-
ident, at last I can have an inaugural ball;
the white house of my corpuscles
asks for new blood; I have given so many transfusions to others
When will you make me your first lady, George?
When will I finally become the first president's wife?

CROSSING THE DELAWARE

the boat
built out of razor blades
moves best on
a burning lake
the grass
twisting itself
into carnation stems; the carnations, thousands of them
burning and making the air smell of hot cracked cinnamon
lake grass waving
from the bottom.
the sand like powdered sugar under your feet,
floating
the hair spread out,
hair speaking the words, "twist me,"
an old pirate doubled up and buried in his treasure chest at the
    bottom
an inch of blue sleeve sticking out by the hinge,
old fishing line gets tangled in my
memories

how come, by the way, you were crossing the Delaware?

It is only when I am tired that I don't believe in war, fighting for
    what
I want. George said, "there can only be peace
when we show that we are ready to fight for it." Well, I am
ready to throw my carnation
burning
into your lap. You're already sitting in that razor blade boat
and if that isn't tricky
I don't know what is,
one little kiss on the forehead for history
is hardly enough. I'll fight to
put my burning flower onto your blazing lake. I'll cross the
    Delaware

with George as escort—military escort—
to get you. I am fascinated by that razor blade boat. I am
delighted by the weapons you use. An elegant battle;
I can't think in pacifist terms any more,
having experienced too many assaults. And I have a secret I'm
   holding
out for you. When we meet in your razor blade boat,
and I am stepping carefully in my bare bare feet,
won't you look in my pocket, notice
what it's lined with—
yes, something to
compliment
your steel.

MONEY OVER THE WATER

What were your textbook motives, I ask my informer balancing
   stars on his eye lids; the motives for throwing that coin, a dollar,
I suppose, across the Potomac?
And he assures me he tried; he threw a quarter over the 1964
   version of that river
         do they get wider or narrower with time lapse
and it sank
with your picture
to the bottom,
George. He said
you did it
for the same reasons
to show that it could be done, crossing the water with
money.

        I crossed crossed crossed the water
        with money,
        money of my lips in the cup of hot coffee,
        money yanked out of my tooth where I hid it when I was
           ten,
        money from baby shoes walking and scratching my palms
           and wrists,
        George
        there is a river between us;
        I was standing on the far shore of the Potomac with an
           Indian
        peering around the tree at me thinking how beautiful
        my silk was, and how ashy blond my hair.
        He was wondering if he could touch my pointed kid shoes
        and bring me to the ceremonial fire to let the whiteness of
           my
        face evoke a buffalo moon. I, not wanting to walk alone
        the wilderness sweeping me like a thorough broom from
           place
        to place,

started. Your dollar coin plunked at my feet,
George, money from across the water
and the Indian sped away in tissue and cellophane fright
knowing that I had the powers of summons
when he saw this sign.
No sign. It wasn't any sign. I was about as far away in time
as tractors
Some old-blooded instinct tells me you can cross with
   money
where you can't cross any other way.
But now swim, George,
the potomac,
or row,
or ride your horse
across.
I want to see you on this side, not just your money.
Ace of Pentacles. You cross me
even when there is no other card

George, I see you most often on money. No wonder I have such an
   obsession.
If you only saw the person you loved in a picture on a coin or a bill
you too would want more and more currency to pass through your
   hands.
What space is there for us to touch in.
We are only connected
by signs.

THE FATHER OF MY COUNTRY

All fathers in Western civilization must have
a military origin. The
ruler,
governor,
yes,
he is
was the
general at one time or other.
And George Washington
won the hearts
of his country—the rough military man
with awkward
sincere
drawing-room manners.

My father;
have you ever heard me speak of him? I seldom
do. But I had a father,
and he had military origins—or my origins from
him
are military,
militant. That is, I remember him only in uniform. But of the navy,
30 years a chief petty officer,
always away from home.

It is rough/ hard for me to speak
now.
I'm not used to talking
about him.
Not used to naming his objects/
objects
that never surrounded me.

A woodpecker with fresh bloody crest
knocks
at my mouth. Father, for the first

time I say
your name. Name rolled in thick Polish parchment scrolls,
name of Roman candle drippings when I sit at my table
alone, each night,
name of naval uniforms and name of
telegrams, name of
coming home from your aircraft carrier,
name of shiny shoes.
name of Hawaiian dolls, name
of mess spoons, name of greasy machinery, and name of
stencilled names.
Is it your blood I carry in a test tube,
my arm,
to let fall, crack, and spill on the sidewalk
in front of the men
I know,
I love,
I know, and
want? So you left my house when I was under two.
being replaced by other machinery (my sister), and
I didn't believe you left me.

         This scene: the trunk yielding treasures of
         a green fountain pen, heart shaped mirror,
         amber beads, old letters with brown ink, and
         the gopher snake stretched across the palm tree
         in the front yard with woody trunk like monkey
           skins,
         and a sunset through the skinny persimmon trees.
           You
         came walking, not even a telegram or post card
           from
         Tahaiti. Love, love, through my heart like ink in
         the thickest nubbed pen, black and flowing into
           words
         You came, to me, and I at least six. Six doilies
         of lace, six battleship cannon, six old beerbottles,
         six thick steaks, six love letters, six clocks

running backwards, six watermelons, and six baby
teeth, a six cornered hat on six men's heads, six
lovers at once or one lover at sixes and sevens;
how I confuse
all this with my
dream
walking the tightrope bridge
with gold knots
over
the mouth of an aenemone/ tissue spiral lips
and holding on so that the ropes burned
as if my wrists had been tied

If George Washington
had not
been the Father
of my Country
it is doubtful that I would ever have
found
a father. Father in my mouth, on my lips, in my
tongue, out of all my womanly fire,
Father I have left in my steel filing cabinet as a name on my birth
certificate, Father I have left in the teeth pulled out at
dentists' offices and thrown into their garbage cans,
Father living in my wide cheekbones and short feet,
Father in my Polish tantrums and my American speech, Father,
    not a
holy name, not a name I cherish but the name I bear, the name
that makes me one of a kind in any phone book because
you changed it, and nobody
but us
has it,
Father who makes me dream in the dead of night of the falling
    cherry
blossoms, Father who makes me know all men will leave me
if I love them,
Father who made me a maverick,

a writer,
a namer,
name/father, sun/father, moon/father, bloody mars/ father,

other children said, "My father is a doctor,"
or
"My father gave me this camera,"
or
"My father took me to
the movies,"
or
"My father and I went swimming,"
but
my father is coming in a letter
once a month
for a while,
and my father
sometimes came in a telegram
but
mostly
my father came to me
in sleep, my father because I dreamed in one night that I dug
through the ash heap in back of the pepper tree and found a
    diamond
shaped like a dog, and my father called the dog and it came leaping
over to him and he walking away out of the yard down the road
    with
the dog jumping and yipping at his heels,

my father was not in the telephone book
in my city;
my father was not sleeping with my mother
at home;
my father did not care if I studied the
piano;
my father did not care what
I did;

and I thought my father was handsome and I loved him and I
   wondered
why
he left me alone so much,
so many years
in fact, but
my father made me what I am,
a lonely woman,
without a purpose, just as I was
a lonely child
without any father. I walked with words, words, and names,
names. Father was not
one of my words.
Father was not
one of my names. But now I say, "George, you have become my
   father,
in his 20th century naval uniform. George Washington, I need your
love; George, I want to call you Father, Father, my Father,"
Father of my country,
that is,
me. And I say the name to chant it. To sing it. To lace it around
me like weaving cloth. Like a happy child on that shining afternoon
in the palmtree sunset with her mother's trunk yielding treasures,
I cry and
cry,
Father,
Father,
Father,
have you really come home?

GEORGE WASHINGTON ABSENT FROM HIS COUNTRY

Your heart,
a sponge lying in the vinegar bowl,
waiting for a dry day
or month
or year
when the corners of the mouth
turn down,
parched as the eyelid of a turtle,

waiting to seep the sour liquid
like the arms of a small squid, calamara,
into the corner of my mouth,
as the sponge is handed up on a long pole
to the criminals dying in a ritual of
crucifixion—remember over 2,000 of them in one month
along the road to Jerusalem;

Your heart, George Washington,
my husband,
which is filled with all the juices I need,
lies somewhere across the Atlantic.
You wanted to be educated in England, as the rest
of your family had been,
but they were too poor when it came round to you,
so you studied at home, became a
surveyor, and finally left,
taking the heart with you, the sponge of vinegar,
that I look for at every ocean.

Perhaps if I could dive under the water,
like a pool ball going into the pocket at the side of the table,
perhaps I would find your heart pumping down there,
perhaps making the waves of some tidal current,
perhaps the liquid that soft sponge contains
would not revive me
in this dry dying period,

when I have been hung up with nails on a piece of wood,
for what I believe, my own angel, very white feathers
telling me there is nothing that love would not cure,

George Washington,
where is that sea flower, that spongy red mass, your heart,
why is it absent from its country,
from me; Mr. President, how could you go away,
with the minutes of the meeting not finished; how could you leave
    me,
a daughter of the American Revolution, standing here
with such a dry mouth, such empty hands that before
touched that heart with fingers, with lips,
why some country in which you can only be crude,
a novelty, at best?

This country has changed since you were its first president;
but not in any real way. We still like the firm jaw,
the determined mouth, the secret ways,
what made us trust you,
a first.

The heart is, of course,
what keeps the body going. The heart
is what keeps time.
All the small feathers you can pick up, even in the woods
of a European country, are not as soft or white
or would mean as much to me
as one smile from you. One trip back across the Atlantic.
Come home, where your spirit
can prevail.

GEORGE WASHINGTON HANDS THE KEYS TO UNCLE SAM

My only defense from your charm is sleep.
                    sleep that rolls pineapple dreams into my arms
                    and makes my hands sticky with juice
Under the flag quilt
I wander off with whiskered cat-fish;
for the 4th of July I take stars out of my blood and put them
in your pocket.

Uncle Sam comes rap rapping at my door.
                    Uncle Sam is the biggest menace of all.
I hide under the flag quilt,
but the fish bother me,
swimming furiously in crowded waters.

George Washington on the phone long distance
tells me to let in my Uncle Sam
and sit on his knee
as I did when I was little

But Uncle Sam has not come to hold me
on his knee.
He has come for my pints of blood
and my war bond savings.
He has come for my pledge of allegiance
and my draft card. He has come for my Ida
Lupino roles
and to make me pay for slavery and the 5th amendment.

Uncle Sam,
my God, you are not my Uncle Sam from Des Moines.
you're a Negro from Durham,
and better educated than I.
Nobody ever told me that Uncle Sam was a Negro.

I'm hiding my blood pints under the bed.
You'll never find my bonds.

My house is locked and only George Washington
has the house keys.
As I say, sleep protects me
from your charms
           the dreams where padlocks are all
           on somebody else
           and it doesn't matter that you have
           all the keys
           now.

UNCLE SAM IN THE WHITE HOUSE

Silver grapes in sleeves
      showering their teeth under feet
        silver tape
  binding the sun, keeping
        it inside my knees
          making my steps shaky

Silver stars taped
  to my lips
      the silver stripes bind me
        each part of my body rests
      wrapped in flags
  in a silvery, sparkling drawer
      sometimes I see my eyes
in the sidewalk.

When Uncle Sam moved into the white house
      the whole country applauded
      its old hero
  and was glad that silver-haired Uncle Sam
      was the first Negro American president.

He redecorated the house in silver
  and my silver knee and elbow bones
      with all their jangling keys
were slipped into his pockets

See how patriotic I am,
  the genuine daughter of
    George Washington,
a silvery key, sometimes a dime or a
  quarter, always a hard little
    click
in the pocket or desk drawer
  of Uncle Sam,

our newly elected Negro president—
                    tiptoe past the silver carpets
outside his door. A little silver ghost
          like a spoon
and he won't let me
          in.

BETWEEN ALL OUR HELLOES & GOODBYES

George Washington
never had a mustache,
though he was
a businessman. He might never
have approved of
the way
you slice my helloes and good-
byes. but you trim
your mustache with the same
razor-
backed clam. keeping your
mouth shut
as he did

Oh. your trimming does not
keep me in shape:
cut cut straight
through the bone
the mustache bone.
the bone helloes that you leave
by the cat's dish.
little ones.

Cut me a tunnel through your
talk. It doesn't
communicate. Cut me in the plain-
est shape

I am in love with
your mustache: it
saves me from saying
I love you
which I wouldn't like
to have to say

in between all our helloes
and goodbyes.

GEORGE WASHINGTON, THE SURVEYOR

Kit of instruments:
   I take the tape measure to my eye
          measure your lips
          how I've measured you so far—

you have an inch of cherry stems in your riddles
two feet of blossoms in your lethal chamber
hundreds of miles in a minor key lining your pallet
a gallon of national law in your name
twenty gross of Gothic letters in your transistor

But I break my measuring stick/ look at all the trees
          we would have to walk over,
look at the rivers and canyons we would have to somehow
              get by,
the measure is a stiff one
          and frightened me away.

BLACK UNCLE SAM AND POOR OFAY ME

My life rides past on a bicycle,
my life is an eagle splashing in the birdbath,
my life is an American eagle with his wings clipped, riding a bicycle,
The story of my life:
I am in love with the eagle
who has flown away with a rabbit dripping.
George Washington takes notes on my life, writing them in
rabbit blood. Somehow the bicycle is an encumbrance.
Uncle Sam enters.

> By this time my life is a map of the United States
> By this time I have no sex, am nothing but a
> piece of paper with a few poems
> written on it: by this time I am in love with
> Uncle Sam but have lost all sense of
> identity; by this time
> I am hysterical with love & hate & confusion:
> And my role comes through to serve me
> historically,
> that American patriot who writes of
> George Washington and Uncle Sam
> may she be nothing more/ old, fat, white . . .

so the feathers sift slowly to the ground as you touch my sleeve,
porches of snow sit on my lap,
closets of silk bolts unroll as I look for you,
my voice is an old mountain hugging your name,

  but I will sing every verse of "The Star Spangled Banner"
  in Latin to avoid talking to you,
and will walk around the whole map to avoid being near you,

153

you who are under my eyelid when I close it,
who have stolen stars from my blood,
who have shot at eagles & slipped them into your
    mouth,
who have frightened me, yes Uncle Sam, with your
    taxes,

and have threatened me with a glittery jail/
my feelings, the glinting bayonet,

a nation at war.

UNCLE SAM & THE GOOD AMERICAN LADY

She rose naked out of the blueberry patch
and when she did her father covered her with shiny tin buckets.

Razzle, dazzle, baby, on the head of your baton,
marching in front of the band,
doing your routine to "Stars & Stripes Forever,"
The Good White American lady with red hair
is in love with Uncle Sam
(and he's not blue; he's black)

Here I am
down in the corner of the painting,
sewing my newest American flag.
I have a dowry of 87 American flags
but am too much in love with George Washington,
my father,
to ever find a husband.
Many tricks with the needle I've developed to get rid of
potential suitors.
I am bad at heart
and often hate my country.
   Take Uncle Sam,
   that Southern Negro who has what they call charm;
   he's not in this picture.
   He's out collecting taxes.
   Uncle Sam's newest tax is on women,
   and it's scandalously high.
   Uncle Sam scares me, and I never pay him my taxes.

   Take that blueberry woman
   with stains on her lips from eating too much;
   that red-haired white Good woman
   who is taxed 80% of her income;
   she's waiting, ready.
   White American women are ready and waiting to be
    taxed
   by that nigger, Uncle Sam.

Idle hands will work for the devil.
So I keep busy,
sewing up my flags
I'm painted here for more than a lifetime.
Love my country; love George,
is my theme song.
Even in this calm picture, I am uneasy—
afraid Uncle Sam will take my 87 dowry flags as tax
and give me no marriage in return.

GEORGE WASHINGTON WRITES HOME ABOUT
HARVESTING HIS HEMP

I won't take a lot of shit
in the name of love.
smoking it,
or eating it,
or shoveling it
for you.

You write a letter to Martha,
telling her how much you miss her,
sitting at home, tight as a cable
managing your house.
How you long to be there
when the plants are harvested,
the special crops you spent long
hours reading the seed catalogue about —
      "makes especially fine
      thick
      resinous
      fibers."
said the book,
so juicy at harvest time
you smell the medicine
in the air.

And so you make special plans to be there
when the hemp is harvested:
your dreams take the form of women
lying down, taking off their clothes
on American flags.
serving you in the name of your country,
the soft aroma of Virgin-
ia hemp curling around your nose
like a cat rubbing at the cook's legs
while she's making dinner.

My first statement is true
about you and me:
the plants are ready to be harvested;
the hemp sticky with brown dust,
as a caterpillar
and you nostalgic,
away from your plantation,
coming in letters to remind
us of your deep commitments there.

But I'll let all that hemp die;
the ropes it will make
mean nothing to me—but nooses.
I will not take any more shit
in the name of love—
not smoke it,
or eat it,
or clean it up for you.

GEORGE WASHINGTON DREAMS OF PARATROOP
FORCES

They all sat in the temporary camp
—no barracks—
the mud had caked them. There was no
soap or hot water.
All cheekbones became high,
apparent.
The winter itself a piece of paper torn & filthy.
George Washington had no shaving mug and his stubble grew
red, gleaming in the moonlight.
                    Marty said he used to be a paratrooper.
                    I asked him if he ever did any sky-diving.
                    Yes, he said, but that was different from
                    ordinary jumping.
                    When you sky-dive you are trying
                    to float, to let
                    arms of wind push you;
                    a General with much brass will put his riding crop
                    under your armpit and
                    tell you to put back your shoulders so the army
                        should
                    see what kind of man you are.
                    Marty said that the first time he
                    was to jump,
                    the men were all lined up at the plane door. He
                    was first in line, and when the
                    door opened, and he took one look down,
                    more than a mile,
                    he didn't have time to panic or think
                    twice
                    because the captain kicked him in the pants and
                    he was on his way down with the parachute
                        bobbing
                    like a golfball,

and the air held him,
loved him
as he's never been loved
by anyone.
I asked him if
he'd read in the paper a few years ago of a
lady sky-diver
whose chute would not open
and who plunged feet first into a lake,
miraculously coming up alive,
unbruised,
unbroken,
and her first words were
"But what did I do wrong," as only
a woman
could be beautifully unperceiving and oblivious
to her luck and her
state of grace.
Washington reading an agricultural manual
and trying to understand why his trees will not root in Virginia soil
knows his men are tired,
discouraged.
They are all potential paratroopers,
wanting to line up in that bent old tinny piano,
wanting to come down over the enemy
and destroy it,
wanting to play soldier in a modern way.
But George, you cannot give them this release,
just as you cannot make your trees grow well.
George, you have skills and powers
we all know about,
and, George, you are a man of action. This is what I like.
George, you could not love or make anything
around you grow,
but you built and pushed and forced
and largely by will
shaped and defended things—real, substantial.

It is this example
I would have you set. Free fall,
the sky dive, being that you use the wind
don't fight it,
but make its purposes yours.
The sky diver,
we cannot say,
is a man who is pushed around by the wind.

The sky diver
is the man who knows both his own mind
and that of the wind.

GEORGE WASHINGTON: THE WHOLE MAN

The disappointment I am talking of now
comes without heartbreak or the
malfunctioning of body and brain,
comes through the hope of communication
and follows the lack of it.
I had hoped you would live up to my idea
of the great man
but found myself disappointed on every level.

I. Reticence   for J.

Sitting at your drawing board
sketching plans for Mt. Vernon
you, as I can remember, fade into that Swede I idealized
Mt. Vernon is typical of the wealthy planter aristocracy style
(or so it says in the book)
and you walk through woods
as tranquilly as/or corridors.
The summer of 1785 brought the
leaf eaters
and tree blight
and no rain. You lost your black gum,
pine,
locust,
poplar,
mulberry,
crab apple,
papaw,
cedar,
hemlock,
and sassafras.
Your imported golden pheasants languished
and when you laid out a deer park,
the deer continually escaped & gnawed away
your saplings.

As much as you worked, your aristocratic lands were
tight-lipped
(much as you are)
communicating not to your fingers. You learned silence
from the torrid summers and the unreachable land
beyond the Alleghenies.
Holding an icy glass
you mediate between desire and responsibility. Like the good
man, you
never choose the easy life.

George, I remember a walk we took through
someone else's lush park
and you asked
how he did it. His fortunes were
in his land, I said,
and you closed your mouth silently
as if it were hinged,
knowing neither your body nor
your land would yield much pleasure,
neither respond to the touch of
a spade or a rake.

We walked over brooks, through
Japonica gardens, and finally to the arched
white gazebo.
Your buckled shoes were dusty and I remember
the tired look as you touched my hand,
lace emerging from your cuff.
We talked of each plant in detail
and yet you never told me
once
anything
about yourself.
The reticence of a man
who had
never learned to talk.

II. The Classical Code   for R.

> "When Lafayette sent him the key of the Bastille, to symbolize
> the overthrow of despotism, Washington responded merely with
> a polite acknowledgement and a token gift in return.
>> Not for the value of the thing, my dear
>> Marquis, but as a memorial, and because
>> they are the manufacture of this city, I
>> send you herewith a pair of shoe-buckles.
> A pair of shoe-buckles—what inspired flatness."

> Marcus Cunliffe, p. 160, GEORGE
>   WASHINGTON,
> MAN AND MONUMENT

and this makes you seem classical, most of all.

I should trim my hair straight across
I should find pleasure in only the straight line.
I should cut out all curves
and melodies
all close connections
and off-beat poses.
I should think of the effect
and should find pleasure only in a
pure
process.
I should designate the goals simply
and be sparing about my sex life.
I should know a great deal
keep it all to myself
and believe in only that which will last.

Shit.
Life upsets those patterns when we are 18/ or at least
my life has.
I want to embrace the ephemeral
as tightly, as spontaneously,
as often
as the historical, classical, and great.
My life is definitely not one long bicycle ride
or one long
anything else.
It is a cold hard fact.
It is true we are too easily impressed
by someone's impeccably good tastes.

George, you did all the right things,
but you hardly seemed alive.
They all said you were dull or hard to talk to,
and of course THAT
isn't classical; so thank god I can
tell you this.
I am pissed off at you for being so easily convinced
by what seem like weak arguments.
Still, it is with pleasure I
remember the shoe-buckles
and with pleasure I see
how you've used Lafayette's key.

III. Pathos   for G.

Whether it is historical or not I cannot say. The protagonist
so to speak was someone famous—
George Washington, to be truthful, who first fell in love with
Betsy Fauntleroy when he was 20
and she, a belle, did not like his manners.
He gave her, I believe,
for I dreamed this and there is no better verifier than the dream,
a glass aquarium containing
18 lizards,
each a different species,

one green sunning itself on a waxy magnolia leaf,
another translucent amber showing the cartilage of the body
as the stick in a clear sucker shows through,
still another black like a tire and rough and contrasting with the
prettiness of the glass and the others.
18 lizards in their glass box.
Hardly calculated to win the embroidered heart of Betsy Fauntleroy,
her powdered wig slipped awry with astonishment
at such a gift.

George, in and out of time, your historical hands
that should sign great documents move over my body,
into my brain,
squeezing the thalamus,
fingering the spongy protrusions that make me dream,
cerebellum, lifting each part away from the other to explore
all the channels, George of many
perceptions, your life
touched me in a way I respond to no one else.
The image, identity of myself;
George, you have come to recite the constitution to me in my sleep.
The word soothe my brain that you earlier explored.

IV. Triumph   for D.

The last time I called the White House and left a message for you
was shortly after you had decided to retire.
You were sitting in your study with the wig off.
You, in fact, had just come from Mexico and an image that the
    public
never discovered was apparent
The snake curling around your neck into your velvet coat,
and the gold Aztec sun trying to draw out your heart with metal
    teeth.
George, you dreamed the sun sucked out your heart
infusing itself with red as it set.
Occasionally, in those last days a cock fight would be set up
in a mahogany room. To bet on the strutter

you had special coins minted,
one side picturing the cock's beak as a weapon in hercules' hand,
the other side giving the eye of the rooster, an eye that
could see into the pocket where it rested,
an eye that would give no rest to anyone that held it.
Transforming your cold life,
the bony moon coming out of the kitchen while sun fills your
    genitals
and begs someone other than Martha to give you one last embrace.
How often we ought to rewrite history,
connections often being made at the wrong time,
facts not consistent with the factors.
George, I would rewrite your history in a hot country
with desert, snakes, and a sip of Rio Grande water.
In triumph we see the great man covered with gold.

P